MACMILLAN MASTER GUIDES

MASTER GUIDES

GENERAL EDITOR: JAMES GIBSON

JANE AUSTEN	*Emma* Norman P...
	Sense and Sensib...
	Persuasion Judy Simons
	Pride and Prejudice Raymond Wilson
	Mansfield Park Richard Wirdnam
SAMUEL BECKETT	*Waiting for Godot* Jennifer Birkett
WILLIAM BLAKE	*Songs of Innocence and Songs of Experience* Alan Tomlinson
ROBERT BOLT	*A Man for All Seasons* Leonard Smith
CHARLOTTE BRONTË	*Jane Eyre* Robert Miles
EMILY BRONTË	*Wuthering Heights* Hilda D. Spear
JOHN BUNYAN	*The Pilgrim's Progress* Beatrice Batson
GEOFFREY CHAUCER	*The Miller's Tale* Michael Alexander
	The Pardoner's Tale Geoffrey Lester
	The Wife of Bath's Tale Nicholas Marsh
	The Knight's Tale Anne Samson
	The Prologue to the Canterbury Tales Nigel Thomas and Richard Swan
JOSEPH CONRAD	*The Secret Agent* Andrew Mayne
CHARLES DICKENS	*Bleak House* Dennis Butts
	Great Expectations Dennis Butts
	Hard Times Norman Page
GEORGE ELIOT	*Middlemarch* Graham Handley
	Silas Marner Graham Handley
	The Mill on the Floss Helen Wheeler
T. S. ELIOT	*Murder in the Cathedral* Paul Lapworth
	Selected Poems Andrew Swarbrick
HENRY FIELDING	*Joseph Andrews* Trevor Johnson
E. M. FORSTER	*A Passage to India* Hilda D. Spear
	Howards End Ian Milligan
WILLIAM GOLDING	*The Spire* Rosemary Sumner
	Lord of the Flies Raymond Wilson
OLIVER GOLDSMITH	*She Stoops to Conquer* Paul Ranger
THOMAS HARDY	*The Mayor of Casterbridge* Ray Evans
	Tess of the d'Urbervilles James Gibson
	Far from the Madding Crowd Colin Temblett-Wood
BEN JONSON	*Volpone* Michael Stout
JOHN KEATS	*Selected Poems* John Garrett
RUDYARD KIPLING	*Kim* Leonée Ormond
PHILIP LARKIN	*The Whitsun Weddings* and *The Less Deceived* Andrew Swarbrick

MACMILLAN MASTER GUIDES

D.H. LAWRENCE	*Sons and Lovers* R. P. Draper
HARPER LEE	*To Kill a Mockingbird* Jean Armstrong
LAURIE LEE	*Cider with Rosie* Brian Tarbitt
GERARD MANLEY HOPKINS	*Selected Poems* R. J. C. Watt
CHRISTOPHER MARLOWE	*Doctor Faustus* David A. Male
THE METAPHYSICAL POETS	Joan van Emden
THOMAS MIDDLETON and WILLIAM ROWLEY	*The Changeling* Tony Bromham
ARTHUR MILLER	*The Crucible* Leonard Smith *Death of a Salesman* Peter Spalding
GEORGE ORWELL	*Animal Farm* Jean Armstrong
WILLIAM SHAKESPEARE	*Richard II* Charles Barber *Othello* Tony Bromham *Hamlet* Jean Brooks *King Lear* Francis Casey *Henry V* Peter Davison *The Winter's Tale* Diana Devlin *Julius Caesar* David Elloway *Macbeth* David Elloway *The Merchant of Venice* A. M. Kinghorn *Measure for Measure* Mark Lilly *Henry IV Part I* Helen Morris *Romeo and Juliet* Helen Morris *A Midsummer Night's Dream* Kenneth Pickering *The Tempest* Kenneth Pickering *Coriolanus* Gordon Williams *Antony and Cleopatra* Martin Wine *Twelfth Night* R. P. Draper
GEORGE BERNARD SHAW	*St Joan* Leonée Ormond
RICHARD SHERIDAN	*The School for Scandal* Paul Ranger *The Rivals* Jeremy Rowe
ALFRED TENNYSON	*In Memoriam* Richard Gill
EDWARD THOMAS	*Selected Poems* Gerald Roberts
ANTHONY TROLLOPE	*Barchester Towers* K. M. Newton
JOHN WEBSTER	*The White Devil* and *The Duchess of Malfi* David A. Male
VIRGINIA WOOLF	*To the Lighthouse* John Mepham *Mrs Dalloway* Julian Pattison
WILLIAM WORDSWORTH	*The Prelude Books I and II* Helen Wheeler

MACMILLAN MASTER GUIDES

THE MAYOR OF CASTERBRIDGE

BY THOMAS HARDY

RAY EVANS

MACMILLAN

First published 1987 by
MACMILLAN PRESS LTD
Houndmills, Basingstoke, Hampshire RG21 6XS
and London
Companies and representatives
throughout the world

ISBN 0–333–40733–4

A catalogue record for this book is available
from the British Library.

12 11 10 9   8   7   6   5
05 04 03 02 01 00 99 98

Printed in Malaysia

CONTENTS

GENERAL EDITOR'S PREFACE

The aim of the Macmillan Master Guides is to help you to appreciate the book you are studying by providing information about it and by suggesting ways of reading and thinking about it which will lead to a fuller understanding. The section on the writer's life and background has been designed to illustrate those aspects of the writer's life which have influenced the work, and to place it in its personal and literary context. The summaries and critical commentary are of special importance in that each brief summary of the action is followed by an examination of the significant critical points. The space which might have been given to repetitive explanatory notes has been devoted to a detailed analysis of the kind of passage which might confront you in an examination. Literary criticism is concerned with both the broader aspects of the work being studied and with its detail. The ideas which meet us in reading a great work of literature, and their relevance to us today, are an essential part of our study, and our Guides look at the thought of their subject in some detail. But just as essential is the craft with which the writer has constructed his work of art, and this may be considered under several technical headings – characterisation, language, style and stagecraft, for example.

The authors of these Guides are all teachers and writers of wide experience, and they have chosen to write about books they admire and know well in the belief that they can communicate their admiration to you. But you yourself must read and know intimately the book you are studying. No one can do that for you. You should see this book as a lamp-post. Use it to shed light, not to lean against. If you know your text and know what it is saying about life, and how it says it, then you will enjoy it, and there is no better way of passing an examination in literature.

JAMES GIBSON

Page numbers throughout these notes refer to the paperback edition of the New Wessex Edition of the novel, with an introduction by Dr F. B. Pinion.

1 THOMAS HARDY: LIFE AND BACKGROUND

Hardy's Wessex is the most strongly-defined of all English fictional regions, Casterbridge, its centre, its most vividly-realized town. This is because Hardy, both in prose and poetry, wrote so powerfully of what he had observed, experienced and inherited as he grew up in the heart of what was to become Wessex. As a young man he moved to London but inevitably returned to Wessex, eventually Dorchester, to produce his finest work.

He was born on 2 June 1840 in the remote hamlet of Higher Bockhampton, three miles east of Dorchester. This was the nearest town and the natural centre of the region. His father, very much a local man, was a master-mason, self-employed and independent, his business fluctuating in size and prosperity; he cared as much for music probably as he did for masonry. Hardy's mother, whose own family had known great hardship, was a very determined woman, adamant that her own children should advance socially. Frequently but without success she urged her husband to move to a better business situation, perhaps in Dorchester. Mr Hardy's business practice was probably more akin to Henchard's than to Farfrae's. Mrs Hardy ensured that her oldest son received an education beyond that which his comparatively humble origins might have indicated. Judging the village school inadequate she sent him to a respected establishment in Dorchester. From the age of ten to sixteen he walked to and fro from Dorchester, becoming increasingly familiar with its streets and people. At sixteen he was articled to John Hicks, a Dorchester architect, eventually lodging in town during the week and spending weekends in the village. His professional status led to contact with the professional classes of the town, including the family of the Reverend Henry Moule, Vicar of Fordington, which became Durnover in the novel and contained Mill Lane, which Hardy would depict so vividly and with such direct knowledge as Mixen Lane. He was to write that his life was a blend of three worlds; the first was one of shepherds and ploughmen in a hamlet outside Dorchester, the second an existence in a county town of assizes and aldermen, the third was that of the student, teaching himself more Greek and Latin in a course of dogged self-improvement. This characteristic finds eventual literary expression in Elizabeth-Jane.

Having completed his training, a restless and ambitious Hardy moved to London in 1862. He was fortunate in establishing himself with a prominent architect, Arthur Blomfield, and a successful career seemed assured. However, his architectural ambitions waned as his dormant leanings towards literature increased. He did not have the stomach for social climbing necessary for advancement and he found the office work mechanical. He lacked qualities he was later to give to Farfrae. By the mid-sixties he was submitting poems, all of which were rejected by publishers.

The sixties of the last century were a period of great intellectual ferment and social controversy. Charles Darwin's *Origin of Species* (1859) was fostering bitter argument, undermining fundamental assumptions and values. The established Church was at war with itself, entrenched dogma under attack from more humanitarian principles. John Stuart Mill's essay on *Liberty* (1859) saw convention as stifling originality and urged an independent stance. Mill also introduced the first women's suffrage bill into Parliament in 1867. The poet Swinburne would excite and shock with his outspoken themes, his fervour and his sweeping rhythms. All were to affect the young Hardy to a considerable degree, emphasizing the sympathetic understanding of the individual, man and woman, and the negative, often harmful results of received conformity.

Yet in 1867 illness and depression took him back to Dorchester. He had been, as was to be the hero of his future novel *The Return of the Native*, a lad of whom much had been expected. Frustrated, he went back to work with Hicks in Dorchester but also began seriously his preferred career as a novelist. He completed his first novel *The Poor Man and the Lady* in 1868. It was an indiscriminate satire on practically every aspect of social life, emphasising the class mesalliance suggested in the title. Publishers recognized the power of the book but it was considered too extreme. The eminent novelist George Meredith advised Hardy to write another novel with a more cohesive plot. *The Poor Man and the Lady* was quarried by Hardy for material later in his career but was never published in its entirety. The second novel, *Desperate Remedies*, was published by Hardy at his own expense in 1871. He lost £15 – a considerable sum in those days – on the endeavour. It is worth looking for the part played by class distinction, and also studying the cohesion of the plot, in *The Mayor of Casterbridge*.

In 1872 *Under the Greenwood Tree* was published, containing the rural parts of his first novel which had been praised by publishers' readers (just as they had condemned the artificiality of his London scenes). This is an early indication of Hardy's powers of creating a living community, based on what he had experienced personally, albeit a community which is giving way to a society in flux.

In 1870, Hicks had asked Hardy to superintend the restoration of St Juliot's Church near Boscastle in Cornwall. Staying at the rectory, he fell in love with the rector's sister-in-law, Emma Lavinia Gifford. She encouraged him in his writing. His third novel, *A Pair of Blue Eyes*, is in part autobiographical but contains sharp comment on arbitrary social distinctions. The 'Poor Man' was still very much alive. Now gaining some critical attention he was invited to write a serial for the prestigious 'Cornhill Magazine'. The result was *Far From the Madding Crowd* which was immensely popular and established Hardy as an important novelist. It was in this novel that he first used the name 'Wessex' and place names in his earlier novels were subsequently amended to fit in with the topography of his adopted region, which developed and became more substantial with each succeeding novel. Casterbridge is the centre and *Far From the Madding Crowd* contains some important Casterbridge scenes. Eventually, Casterbridge will emerge as the centre of its own novel.

The success of his fourth novel gave him some financial security and enabled him to marry Emma Gifford. There was also an expectation that Hardy would go on writing comfortably rural novels which a largely urban reading class would always welcome. However, he refused to be typecast and during a ten year period of movement from Dorset to London and back to Dorset his published work included a satirical study of London life and class relationships 'The Hand of Ethelberta' and, by far the greatest achievement, *The Return of the Native*, a sombre but compelling study of thwarted relationships in the isolated Wessex community of Egdon Heath. The landscape was drawn in part from the heathland stretching away behind Hardy's birth-place. He wrote most effectively of that which he knew most intimately. In June 1883 the Hardys returned to settle in Dorchester, where *The Mayor of Casterbridge* was begun in 1884 and completed by April 1885. It was serialised weekly in *The Graphic* in 1886 and subsequently published.

In 1885, Thomas and Emma (sadly, there were no children) moved into their newly-built house, Max Gate, on the outskirts of Dorchester. They made frequent visits to London, Hardy's reputation as a novelist enabling him to mix with the literary and socially famous. The mason's son from the remote hamlet had achieved a great deal more than what had been expected of him. Unhappily his marriage seemed to be less successful. His wife accompanied him less and less on the London visits, at home there was estrangement. Biographers argue over the harmony, or lack of it, in the marriage during these years at Max Gate.

What is clear is that the tone of Hardy's novels became increasingly sombre. *Tess of the D'Urbervilles* (1891) and *Jude the Obscure* (1896), while extending the geographical Wessex to its territorial limits, dealt with two uprooted, wandering characters who attract to themselves all the prejudice and hostility of a rigidly conventional public. Hardy's attack on convention produced sharp counter-attacks; he was criticised for immorality and heresy, his views on marriage exciting particular condemnation. He turned from novels back to poetry, his first love, and published *Wessex Poems* in 1898. These included some with a Casterbridge setting.

He continued to write poetry, and his epic of the Napoleonic War, *The Dynasts*, was published between 1903 and 1908. His reputation grew as a novelist and poet. He refused a knighthood in 1908 but became a member of the exclusive Order of Merit in 1910 and, somewhat tardily, was made a Freeman of the town of Dorchester in the same year. Casterbridge had seemed reluctant to honour its own.

In 1912 Emma Hardy died unexpectedly. Moved by a complexity of emotions, Hardy wrote in her memory some of the finest love poems in the language.

Florence Dugdale, very much younger than Hardy, had been acting as secretary to him for several years. In 1914 they married and a final period of Hardy's life opened during which Max Gate was to become a visiting place for a great many of the established and up-and-coming writers of the day, as diverse as H. G. Wells, Virginia Woolf, Siegfried Sassoon and Lawrence of Arabia. He went on writing poetry and planned to produce a volume on his ninetieth birthday, but became increasingly disillusioned with the development of the so-called civilised world. The Great War was a shattering revelation of the lack of loving-kindness between individuals which he prized as mankind's only salvation and which seemed to become less and less universal. Hardy died in 1928, his ashes honoured with a state funeral in Westminster Abbey, his heart buried in Stinsford churchyard, near Dorchester, in the grave of his first wife.

2 PLOT SYNOPSIS

Sometime in the 1820s, Michael Henchard, a young hay-trusser, with Susan his wife, and baby daughter, Elizabeth-Jane, trudges through Wessex, searching for work. At Weydon-Priors' Fair, Henchard, in a drunken stupor, auctions his wife to a sailor, Richard Newson, who takes wife and baby away with him. Afterwards, Henchard unsuccessfully searches for them, vowing to avoid alcohol for twenty-one years. He finally arrives at Casterbridge. Nineteen years later Susan with her eighteen-year old daughter by Newson, the second Elizabeth-Jane, returns to Weydon-Priors. Henchard's baby had died. Newson was feared lost at sea and Susan was seeking Henchard, hoping for help. They discover him in Casterbridge, a thriving corn merchant and the town's Mayor, though in some difficulty with over-ripe wheat. At the same time a young and charismatic Scotsman, Donald Farfrae, is in Casterbridge, bound for Canada. He stays overnight in the same inn as Susan and Elizabeth-Jane, who finds him attractive.

Farfrae generously shows Henchard a method of part-restoring poor wheat. Henchard, attracted by the newcomer's personality, persuades him to become manager of his business, although he had previously offered the post to another man, Joshua Jopp. The next morning, Susan sends Elizabeth-Jane to Henchard, to announce their arrival. Henchard is most affected and assumes Elizabeth-Jane is his own daughter, realising gratefully that Susan had kept the auction a secret from her. At an evening meeting in the Roman amphitheatre, Susan agrees to Henchard's plan that they should re-marry, Elizabeth-Jane thus becoming his legal step-daughter, though Susan allows him to go on believing that she is his natural daughter.

Henchard, grateful for Farfrae's companionship, confides in him the details of the auction and Susan's return. He also tells him of a former relationship with a young woman, Lucetta Le Sueur, who had cared for him when he was ill. In some distress she had written compromising letters to him after he had left Jersey. Believing Susan dead, he had promised marriage to Lucetta. Farfrae drafts a letter for him breaking the engagement.

After a discreet interval Henchard marries Susan and does his best to make her and Elizabeth-Jane happy, taking pride in Elizabeth-Jane's attractiveness and intelligence, and suggesting that she take the name of Henchard, though Susan prevents this. Henchard's reliance on Farfrae as friend and business manager increases, while Farfrae is attracted to Elizabeth-Jane. Susan plots to bring them together.

The developing relationships receive sudden checks. Farfrae successfully challenges Henchard's bullying of a workman, Abel Whittle. His prestige in Casterbridge increases and he leads the organisation of a holiday celebration. Henchard's rival celebration proves a fiasco and he dismisses Farfrae in a fit of jealousy. Farfrae promptly becomes Henchard's business rival, causing him to forbid the budding relationship with Elizabeth-Jane.

Susan falls ill and during the illness an unexpected letter tells Henchard that Lucetta will pass through Casterbridge, hoping to collect her incriminating letters. Her aunt's death causes Lucetta to miss Henchard and the letters; she inherits her aunt's fortune and name of Templeman. Susan dies leaving Henchard a letter to be opened only on Elizabeth-Jane's wedding day. The lonely Henchard turns to Elizabeth-Jane, revealing enough of the past to convince her that he is her natural father. However, his reading of Susan's imperfectly-sealed letter reveals that Newson is the father, a dramatic shock to Henchard (and to the reader)! He maintains his position as father but the developing love becomes dislike. He encourages Farfrae to see Elizabeth-Jane, now completely at a loss and very much alone.

Meanwhile, Lucetta moves to High-Place Hall in Casterbridge, still hoping to marry Henchard. Elizabeth-Jane happily becomes the companion to this apparently sophisticated woman. Because of Henchard's delay, Lucetta's affection cools. She meets and falls in love with Farfrae, who, ironically, had been seeking Elizabeth-Jane. Henchard is incensed and engages Jopp as manager to help ruin Farfrae by highly competitive trade. Instead, their speculative plans are ruined by the weather, Farfrae prospers even more while Henchard faces crippling losses. Jopp is summarily dismissed. Inadvertently Henchard overhears Lucetta and Farfrae discuss marriage; immediately he calls on Lucetta and in Elizabeth-Jane's presence compels Lucetta to agree to marry him.

At this crisis in his affairs, the secret of the auction is disclosed in the Casterbridge courtroom by the furmity woman from Weydon-Priors. Lucetta now regards her promise as void and marries Farfrae. Henchard is outraged at the broken promise and threatens to disclose his previous relationship with Lucetta. Elizabeth-Jane feels completely isolated and finds lodgings for herself. Henchard, too, becomes isolated as he declines into bankruptcy, eventually finding seedy lodgings with Jopp and thinking of emigration. Farfrae attempts a reconciliation but Henchard falls ill. Elizabeth-Jane emerges to nurse him as her father and at last he begins to appreciate her worth. Philosophically, he begins working for Farfrae as a hay-trusser in the yard he once owned. The news that Farfrae might be Mayor, coupled with brooding on the loss of Lucetta, brings back his hatred. When his temperance vow expires he begins drinking heavily, publicly threatening revenge. Meanwhile, Farfrae, who is trying to help Henchard, becomes Mayor, a final blow to Henchard's pride.

Lucetta still seeks her letters, left by Henchard in his old safe. Henchard collects them, reads extracts to Farfrae but cannot disclose the signature. He promises the letters to Lucetta but unwisely asks Jopp, affronted by Lucetta, to deliver them. He takes them to Peter's Finger, where they are read by the disreputable frequenters of the inn and judged sufficient evidence for a skimmington ride to shame Lucetta and Henchard. Lucetta does receive the letters, destroying them and thinking herself finally secure.

At the reception for a royal personage, Farfrae's first important duty as Mayor, a drunken and dishevelled Henchard intrudes and is pushed back by Farfrae. Following this final provocation Henchard decoys Farfrae to the top of his own granary, planning to fight and kill him, though with one arm tied to make the contest equal. In the fight he had Farfrae at his mercy but allows him to leave. Seeking composure, Farfrae turns to a business appointment in Budworth but an unexpected summons to Weatherbury in the opposite direction ensures that he misses the skimmington ride. Lucetta sees the effigies of herself and Henchard from her window and collapses in an epileptic fit. A distraught Henchard finds Farfrae to persuade him to go home immediately but is rebuffed, Farfrae not arriving until later, when Lucetta has not long to live.

Henchard now hopes for some happiness with Elizabeth-Jane; he desperately needs her love. The hope is thwarted by the appearance of Newson seeking news of his family. A shattered Henchard tells him that both Elizabeth-Jane and Susan are dead. Newson accepts this and leaves Casterbridge but, terrified by grief and apprehension, Henchard contemplates suicide. However, his effigy 'drowned' in the river seems to indicate to him that he should live. For a short time he does enjoy a calm existence with Elizabeth-Jane but this is disturbed by Farfrae's renewed attention to her. When Newson re-appears, Henchard leaves Casterbridge – and a mystified and sorry Elizabeth-Jane – before his deceit can be revealed. Elizabeth-Jane is re-united with her real father and the wedding with Farfrae is planned.

Henchard leads a lonely, self-accusing life as a hay-trusser, desperate for news of Elizabeth-Jane. Hearing of the wedding he goes to Casterbridge with a caged goldfinch as a present. At this meeting a distressed Elizabeth-Jane cannot forgive his deception of her father, rejecting Henchard who sadly returns the way he had come.

The girl bitterly regrets her coldness when the abandoned birdcage is found. She persuades Farfrae to initiate a prolonged search but Henchard has vanished. Ultimately they discover Abel Whittle sadly attending Henchard's body in a derelict cottage. Movingly, he tells them of Henchard's last journey and death. Henchard's bitter will is intended to obliterate all memory of him. In what amounts to an epilogue Elizabeth-Jane grows into an admirably balanced person.

3 SUMMARIES AND CRITICAL COMMENTARY

Chapter One is given a more extended commentary than subsequent chapters to draw attention to the manner in which every part of a chapter contributes to the variety, power and interest of the whole.

CHAPTER 1

Summary

Late one summer evening, a young man with his wife and baby girl are wearily approaching the village of Weydon Priors in Upper Wessex. The family trudge in silence. The man, who has the gait of a skilled country-man, is looking for work and accommodation, but both are unobtainable. There is a fair in the village and they seek refreshment, the woman diverting the man from the beer tent to the innocuous furmity tent. Ironically, the furmity is laced with smuggled rum and the man becomes increasingly truculent and inebriated. He declaims upon the limitations of marriage and prompted by a sale outside the tent impulsively offers his wife for auction. What seemed to begin as a drunken gesture becomes grim reality as he determinedly raises his price to five guineas. Abruptly, to general surprise, a passing sailor accepts and the money changes hands. The sailor leaves with the woman and child, Elizabeth-Jane. The man, shaken but unrepentant, is left to spend the night sleeping off his drunkenness in the tent.

Commentary

The chapter, part of a prologue to the novel proper, begins with a favourite Hardy image, movement across a wide landscape, with the emphasis here on the long day's journey of the man, woman and baby, a family unit. They are not vagrants but are forced to wander in search of work and a home. Hardy's Wessex at this time offers an uncertain livelihood, even to skilled countrymen. In fact Wessex is very much a world in transition where these initial scenes of movement set the restless tone: it is a world of increasing social mobility with the tensions of social rise and fall inherent in the succeeding drama.

The anonymous main character is in part representative of the skilled countrymen who are victims of economic laws. The economic factor is a vital part of the novel's background. In Weydon Priors we can assume that uncertain harvests have meant that work is scarce, houses demolished and more families on the road.

The young hay-trusser, however, is no anonymous symbol, but an individual of character emphasised from the start, stern, dogged, phlegmatic, perverse, a mixture of strength and weakness. There is an early hint of his isolation and indifference to the world. The silence of his family group is uncanny, with no dialogue at all for almost three pages. Instead the unnatural domestic situation is emphasised by gesture. A metaphysical dimension is introduced with ironic comment on the effect of civilisation on the woman's natural attitude and expression; with her the unfair bias of Time and Chance have hardened natural liveliness to apathy. In this world human beings seem the victims of indiscriminate forces.

The fair, where a lively section of society is enjoying itself, is central to the chapter. Festivities, an important part of community life, are to be significant in the novel. There are no frivolities for the travellers but only the need for refreshment. A hint of an all-important weakness is given when the man is diverted from the beer tent. The furmity woman dominates her tent, outwardly white and dispensing health but, with her cauldron, suggesting the role of a white witch. The furmity tent is the opposite of wholesome; its spells come from smuggled rum, another example to convince the wife of the irony of circumstances.

Like almost everything else in the chapter, the gossip in the tent centres on marriage, the basis of society. The hay-trusser, very determined in his drinking, a man of no half-measures, argues that marriage has prevented his success in the fodder business. Fate again intervenes with the auctioneer's voice outside the tent heralding the auction within. The scene is not hurried, the maximum dramatic effect is obtained as the auction proceeds only half-seriously. There are long pauses, Hardy is precise on time here, while the befuddled man broods on his proposition with his wife increasingly distraught and then bitter. This drunken game is not new.

We accept the auction because of the vividness and air of verisimilitude of the preceding paragraphs and the careful build-up in the tent. We accept the highly improbable second wanderer, humanised by his gentle smile. His money on the table electrifies the atmosphere in the tent, the first of many commentaries on the power and ambiguous influence of money.

The woman rebels at last, the man cannot bear to be challenged and is incapable at this stage of any magnanimity.

He becomes almost comic in his bewilderment, an object of laughter. Still in character, he then shrugs the matter off, blaming his wife for her vagaries but regretting the loss of the child, though still as a piece of personal property. There seems little capacity for love in the man of character. As his family walk out of his life he is left very much alone.

The natural world is used throughout the chapter to give a critical counterpoint to human activities. Dying leaves and weak birds seem to echo the faded relationship of the plodding travellers. The measured rhythm of the seasons will bring leaves and birdsong back but what is the destiny of the human being? The swallow is trapped momentarily in the tent but escapes to migrate to happier climes. Are the man and his family trapped in the tent and are their actions to have inevitable repercussions which they cannot avoid? The gentle horses suggest a natural harmony absent from the human species: the peace and beauty of the sunset, after the squalid and inhuman end of the hay-trusser's marriage, question the concept of man as the pinnacle of creation. Yet it is with man that the story must deal and there is a portent in the reminder that weather can change dramatically. The trusser's prosperity will depend on the weather.

This is an intensely visual novel. Hardy's language conjures up scenes of cinematic vividness, as with the long shot of the travellers approaching Weydon, zooming into the man's square profile, moving down his body to emphasize the dogged movement by the folds of the trouser legs. There is the bustling variety of the fairground in the evening light, contrasted with subdued atmosphere and sense of confinement of the tent's interior. The word positioning and rhythm of the prose emphasise movement and meaning, illustrated by the heaviness and remoteness of 'she plodded on in the shade of the hedge, silently thinking' or the casual but strong suggestion of shared life in 'the low easy, confidential chat of people full of reciprocity'. The last paragraph of the chapter is a fine example of varied sentence structure, with an ebbing movement leading to the simple but beautifully modulated final sentence which brings everything to an end.

CHAPTER 2

Summary

The young man awakens early next morning in an empty furmity tent. Finding his wife's wedding ring on the floor and the sailor's money in his pocket convinces him that the auction took place. With very mixed emotions he decides to follow his initial impulse to find his family and endure any consequences. To emphasise his resolution he vows to renounce strong drink for twenty-one years, his own age, revealing that his name is Michael Henchard. He searches for months but hears eventually that the family had emigrated to Canada. He comes to a decision and travels doggedly to Casterbridge.

Commentary

Henchard looks out on to a most evocative and varied landscape. Hardy repeatedly contrasts the forms and rhythms of landscape with the vicissitudes of his human characters who traverse its permanence.

The chapter develops Henchard's character. He is confirmed as impetuous, liable to outbreaks of irrational rage and subsequent, baffled, self-justification. Yet there are redeeming features; he does feel ashamed and accepts the responsibility of rectifying the situation. Lonely pride struggles with the urge to do the right thing. He spends the sailor's money reluctantly. Everything must be done with determination bordering on vehemence.

CHAPTER 3

Summary

The first two chapters form a prologue to the novel proper. Some nineteen years later, the erstwhile Susan Henchard, now Newson, is walking the same dusty road to Weydon Priors, accompanied by a grown-up Elizabeth-Jane. Newson is presumed drowned at sea. Repeating a pattern, they turn aside into the fair. Susan finds the old furmity woman, more witch-like and almost destitute, selling very inferior furmity though still flavoured with smuggled rum. The woman informs Susan that Henchard returned to the fair and asked her to tell anyone enquiring that he was going to Casterbridge. Susan and Elizabeth-Jane set off for Casterbridge.

Commentary

Hardy begins by emphasising the passage of time, with attendant changes. The traditional business of the great country fair is in decline, a symptom of a change in rural economic patterns. The furmity woman's customers have declined to small boys with halfpennies.

The two women begin to emerge; there is obviously a very strong bond between mother and daughter. We believe Elizabeth-Jane to be Henchard's child though clearly she knows nothing of the auction. There is irony in her half-interested enquiries about him; her innocent question to Susan anticipates a major plot complication.

Elizabeth-Jane is keen that they are 'respectable' in all they do, reminding us of a world of social distinctions, while Henchard's returning to the fair a year after selling his wife indicates the length and tenacity of his search.

CHAPTER 4

Summary

The beginning of the chapter explains the presence of Susan and Elizabeth-Jane at the fair. Newson had taken Susan and the baby to Canada. About twelve years later, they returned to Falmouth. Susan had accepted the legality of the auction but had always hesitated to tell Elizabeth-Jane. Eventually, however, she is advised that there is no legal basis to her relationship with Newson. The latter's reported loss at sea solved the immediate problem of what to do. Susan was very much aware that Elizabeth-Jane wished to better herself but 'the strait-waistcoat of poverty' (p. 57) threatened to deny the girl's potential. She decides to seek out Henchard but not to reveal her previous relationship with him.

Commentary

The move to Casterbridge inaugurates the action proper. Susan's simple but determined reactions to life are instanced in her religious acceptance of Newson for many happy years, only to be followed by her equally firm doubts. Newson's loss is convenient. As he walked by chance into the furmity tent, so he can be reported lost by chance at sea in order to advance the plot. Elizabeth-Jane is established as a character with her own personality, undeveloped as yet but with both physical and mental potential. Susan's poor health may suggest that the plot requires her death, once her mission has been accomplished.

The introduction to Casterbridge is a marvellous mixture of sight and sound. There is a cinematic distance shot from a hedge-bank, giving a medieval compactness to the 'old-fashioned' town and its tree-lined walks, gleaming in the setting sun. The way in is through tunnelled darkness, emerging into glittering lamplight which offers a sense of warmth and safety. A mass of detail emphasises the agricultural bias of the shops, suggesting a prosperous High Street commercial life. The intricate detail of the church tower establishes that building very firmly. The sound of curfew clocks chiming in sequence reminds the reader that this is part of a pattern of social life, that Susan and Elizabeth-Jane are moving into a community. The novel has hitherto had a nomadic life; here it can settle and develop.

Yet all is not quite well in the community. Two men are arguing over Henchard. He is in Casterbridge but from the beginning seems a source of contention. Also there is a crisis over bread. The 'poor folks' spokeswoman makes this clear.

CHAPTER 5

Summary

The town band attracts mother and daughter to 'The King's Arms', the principal hotel in Casterbridge. A crowd of the less prosperous citizens gazes through the open window at the lavish public dinner inside, presided over by the Mayor. The women react in different ways to the information that the Mayor is Henchard, their kinsman. We learn that he has been in Casterbridge nineteen years and that the facts of his teetotal oath and remarkable rise to civic prominence are common gossip.

Commentary

The re-appearance of Henchard, last seen as an out-of-work hay-trusser and now resplendent as the leading citizen of a thriving urban community, is a dramatic shock. He is introduced at the height of his powers, dominating the guests within and the crowd without, everyone hanging on his words. The shortcomings of the young man in the furmity tent seem to have been disciplined by age and experience but it is emphasised that the impulsive temper is still dormant, under a composure that is only skin-deep.

He is isolated as the leading character on the stage. Is it however a convivial banquet for him? The audience includes all the social strata of Casterbridge: the rich guests who are the public worthies, the lesser tradesmen and the commoners, in and out of work, who are happy to gather for any social occasion. Henchard himself has worked his way from a penniless wanderer to an established tycoon. Social distinctions are carefully drawn.

The poorer people, to whom gossip and scandal are a way of life, are used by Hardy to give us the general knowledge of what is going on in the town. It is a convenient method of passing on necessary information. They know that Henchard is under pressure, that he has bought and sold sub-standard wheat. Henchard has built a commercial empire which has proved too big for him – we do not yet know why – and the mistakes are all too apparent. Henchard, barely controlling his temper, admits his errors, though he can always emphasise the dependence on the weather. He has advertised for a manager, which is a step vital for the development of the plot.

Susan thinks of the furmity tent and the former Henchard, thus emphasising the distance he has travelled. Hardy makes sure that the time sequence is remembered. Henchard's vow had two years to run, hence nineteen years have passed. We are reminded twice that Elizabeth-Jane is eighteen, a significant fact for the novel's development.

CHAPTER 6

Summary

Donald Farfrae is passing through Casterbridge and overhears the critical questioning of the Mayor concerning the poor wheat and his defiant assertion that it cannot be used. Acting on impulse he sends Henchard a note and then goes on to 'The Three Mariners', intending to spend one night in Casterbridge. Susan and Elizabeth-Jane also decide to stay at the inn. Henchard, very pre-occupied with Farfrae's note, eventually goes to the inn in search of the stranger who sent him the message.

Commentary

Coincidence brings Farfrae into Casterbridge and contact with Henchard at the precise moment the latter is doggedly accepting a reversal that Farfrae knows he can remedy. It must seem like benevolent good fortune to Henchard. Farfrae, like Henchard before him, and latterly Susan and Elizabeth-Jane, is a wanderer. Like Henchard, he seeks work. As opposed to the massive and florid Henchard, he is 'a young man of remarkably pleasant aspect'. He has a smart bag but seems by no means rich for he seeks a modestly-priced inn. Inns are used by Hardy as indicators of social class. Henchard and Farfrae inhabit different worlds; 'The King's Arms' is above 'The Three Mariners' in its location, status and clientele. Yet Henchard too once walked into Casterbridge, a stranger and without work.

The almost tangible creation of Casterbridge is carried on with Hardy's description of 'The Three Mariners'. We have a very solid impression of the exterior with its amusingly-depicted sign. Hardy allows us to peep through the shutters at a ritualistic scene, part of the pattern of Casterbridge life. Will other patterns emerge as the novel continues?

CHAPTER 7

Summary

Elizabeth-Jane, working to reduce lodging expenses, takes in Farfrae's supper but, though she admired his attractive features, he remains unaware of her. She and Susan overhear Henchard's first conversation with Farfrae. Henchard has confused Farfrae with Joshua Jopp, who had applied for the manager's job. Henchard is rapidly impressed by Farfrae, who generously gives him the wheat-restoring process. He offers Farfrae the manager's position but Farfrae, with his heart set on America, reluctantly refuses it. Henchard and Farfrae obviously warm to each other but it seems they will part – Casterbridge is not Farfrae's world.

Commentary

For the first time the four principal characters are all together in one building and the interweaving of their lives begins. For Elizabeth-Jane respectability seems her only concern. She strikes us as rather prim on first acquaintance, rather 'old-fashioned' herself, though that is how she had described Casterbridge! At least she is resourceful. Susan is in the background, almost always apprehensive. The two male protagonists are shown in sharp contrast, both physically and mentally. It is the prospect of improving his poor wheat which has brought Henchard to Farfrae's room, but in the domestic intimacy something more than a business contact develops. Hardy uses another favourite device here, the overheard conversation. We learn that Henchard is a very tall man and that he values this, but also that he is prepared to admit his lack of organisational skills. Farfrae is slighter physically but obviously has the manner of a matter-of-fact, precise businessman, impressive to deal with and leaving nothing to chance. He is also moved by Henchard's genuine warmth – is there anywhere else in the novel where Henchard talks of his relatives outside marriage? A relationship has begun though it appears impermanent. The situation is ironic in the light of Henchard's disenchantment later.

CHAPTER 8

Summary

The public room of 'The Three Mariners' is described, filled with a broad cross-section of Casterbridge's regular drinkers. Farfrae joins them and sings several songs which captivate his audience, including a concealed Elizabeth-Jane. Henchard listens from the street.

Commentary

This almost static chapter serves to indicate Farfrae's entry into Casterbridge and initiates his conquest of that society. The interior scene contrasts sharply with that observed in 'The King's Arms'. That was open to the world, ostentatious and formal, with supercilious waiters looking on. Here the windows are shuttered and a comfortably familiar atmosphere prevails. There is class distinction: the drinkers range from master-trades-men to the lower orders of Casterbridge. Detail emphasises the difference, from privileged window-seats to rough benches, or glasses to rough cups. The lower orders also drink in semi-darkness. Yet these lesser citizens of Casterbridge have a vital part to play in the novel and add immeasurably to the vitality of the general picture of the town.

Into this critical chorus Farfrae intrudes an alien presence but makes himself at home very soon. Compare Henchard's difficulty in putting other people at their ease. The enthusiasm and spontaneity of his singing appeal to emotions that the business-like town subdues in its everyday life, though Christopher Coney breaks the romantic illusion with his question and comment.

Elizabeth-Jane's character is being developed also. She is seldom far away when any significant development is taking place. She is impressed by the Scotsman's seriousness and strength of purpose. Though she is so young her philosophy is a sombre one; either through temperament or experience she has become a stoic.

A sad footnote to the gaiety within has Henchard pacing alone in an empty High Street, emphasising his isolation from any informal social life in Casterbridge, and his essential loneliness. He listens for a long time. Everyone in the chapter regrets the imminent departure of the stranger who has captivated Casterbridge.

CHAPTER 9

Summary

Farfrae is escorted by Henchard to the Bristol Road with the latter still attempting to persuade him to stay. Elizabeth-Jane is sent by Susan to seek Henchard, traversing the length of the High Street as she does so. This is described with immense wealth of detail. She reaches Henchard's house and finds Farfrae in his office. A flash-back relates how Henchard finally persuaded him and then could not do enough for him.

Commentary

The chapter is skilfully constructed to allow the three characters to develop the plot as they walk through a crowded Casterbridge. Their lives are becoming inter-twined against the background of all the interconnecting activities that make up the life of the county town. The town is established as the logical centre of the area; the growing and harvesting in the fields around is complemented by the buying and selling within. Corn is its life-blood and reason for existence. Its architecture reflects long-established prosperity, with the old houses offering glimpses of traditional gardens. The house fronts look on to the variety and liveliness of the present. An almost tangible sense of congestion is realised with carts from many parts of Wessex, animals and human beings thronging the street. Loaded Henchard waggons remind us of the most prosperous man in the town.

   Elizabeth-Jane, seeking Henchard, finds Farfrae. This is an effective dramatic surprise. Has a night's reflection modified his resolve? He seems very much at home in Henchard's office. He is also brought into constant contact with Elizabeth-Jane. Are the two being linked in the reader's imagination?

   Characteristically, Henchard has persisted and achieved his purpose. Equally characteristically, he helps Farfrae to an enormous breakfast and insists on taking all his decisions for him. 'Overwhelming' seems the correct adjective for Henchard.

CHAPTER 10

Summary

Henchard peremptorily dismisses Jopp, who presumed that he had been appointed manager. Elizabeth-Jane introduces herself to Henchard as the daughter of Susan Newson. Henchard welcomes her warmly and arrranges a meeting with her mother.

Commentary

The dismissal of Jopp, who had a legitimate claim to the manager's position, contrasts sharply with the prolonged discussions attendant on Farfrae's appointment. Henchard has decided and will not change his mind, but the business ethics are dubious and he has made an enemy. The reception of Elizabeth-Jane could not be more contrasting. Elizabeth-Jane's direct and unsuspecting words reduce the normally loquacious Henchard almost to incoherence – his conversation is punctuated by dashes! The fact that Susan has not revealed the auction secret amazes him. He is genuinely moved, a quieter, subdued Henchard, acting with an uncharacteristic delicacy of manner. He becomes increasingly moved as the conversation proceeds, wincing as she calls Newson 'father'. Already he accepts her as his daughter and is jealous that this is not recognised. For the only time we see Henchard close to tears. Even in the most tender scene, however, the commercial ethos of Casterbridge is never far away. The five guineas he sends represents the symbolic buying back of a wife, and the bonus acquisition of a grown-up daughter. It is a well intentioned gesture but smacks of the completion of a business transaction; money can put all things right.

His mood can change abruptly from the sublime to the deeply suspicious. Is Elizabeth-Jane an imposter? Obviously, as she is not his daughter, the irony is complex. Her bearing, however, has already established her as absolutely without guile. Henchard's world has been transformed. 'Excitement' in living is an unusual experience for him. Into his loneliness has come family and friend. He is too excited to cope with everything at once but the practical Farfrae pauses only to wonder and then gets on immediately with his new work.

CHAPTER 11

Summary

The meeting between Henchard and Susan takes place in the Roman amphitheatre on the outskirts of Casterbridge. The arena, with its cruel associations, is described in detail, Hardy going on to emphasise the Roman ancestry of the town. Against the background of the intimidating atmosphere, Henchard suggests that Susan and her daughter rent a cottage in Casterbridge, to be followed in due course by his re-marrying Susan, Elizabeth-Jane to live with them as his apparent step-daughter. Susan agrees.

Commentary

The secret meeting with Susan must take place away from the familiar lights of the town. Henchard has been forced to frequent the most forbidding spot in Casterbridge. Hardy's imagination had obviously been captured by this spot, mounds of earth indicating that a town had been established and people entertained almost two thousand years ago. and through the centuries since. Casterbridge gains an historic perspective. Does this contribute to our interest?

Man is also placed in perspective against the permanence of the monument. His activities are transitory; heroic or brutal, the amphitheatre has brooded over them all, inevitably bounded by death. A scene from Henchard's life drama is to be played here. Is his striving to fulfil his own destiny to culminate in a public spectacle?

CHAPTER 12

Summary

Henchard returns home to find Farfrae still at work reducing the chaos of Henchard's bookkeeping to order. He entertains Farfrae and then tells him not only the story of the sale of his wife but also of his much later involvement with a young woman in Jersey, whom he had then promised to marry. He is determined to stand by Susan and asks Farfrae's help in drafting a letter of apology and resignation to the woman in Jersey. When the letter is posted Henchard hopes, though with some misgiving, that his matrimonial affairs can be settled satisfactorily. He adds a substantial cheque to the letter to Jersey.

Commentary

The initial emphasis in the chapter is placed on the business qualities of Donald Farfrae, his patience, admirable attention to detail and disregard of working to the clock. The contrast with Henchard is again brought out. Henchard has no time for the methodical accounting on which an up-to-date business has to be founded. He grudgingly acknowledges mental skills, but for him business success lies in personal cut and thrust. Yet the two men, mutual opposites, are drawn together and Henchard takes Farfrae completely into his confidence. He has entered a new world of intimate personal relationships. A positive side to Henchard's character is shown by his concern to make amends to the Jersey woman. Money is to be the means, thus involving the commercial ethos of the book; money buys back a wife but also buys off a mistress. This unexpected introduction of another female character adds a further twist and potential to the plot. Is the introduction convincing? Henchard seems poised at the start of a new life.

CHAPTER 13

Summary

Henchard settles Susan and Elizabeth-Jane in a cottage in Casterbridge, sparing no expense in order to make them comfortable. He visits frequently and soon the marriage ceremony takes place in Casterbridge Church. A crowd of the poorer classes gathers outside the church and acts as a good-humoured chorus to the proceedings, very much aware of the discrepancy in fortunes and status between bride and groom. Anecdotes from other more riotous marriages are exchanged.

Commentary

Henchard throws himself into his new plans with great enthusiasm. The word 'business' and the phrase 'business-like determination' do suggest a material transaction rather than an affectionate ceremony, but the incidental details of the furniture emphasise that nothing money can buy is omitted. He feels remorse for the treatment of Susan but Elizabeth-Jane is a more potent force motivating him. She has impressed him and this will be the beginning of a see-saw relationship between them. There is too the hint of masochism; Henchard will punish himself by shedding something of the Mayoral dignity by the marriage.

The urban chorus seizes upon this point immediately though not unkindly. Their stories add a further blend of life in and around Casterbridge, being the stuff of which folklore is made. Farfrae, rapidly becoming indispensable, assists at the wedding.

The chapter opens with a fine atmospheric paragraph depicting Susan's cottage in the autumn evening, with the view looking out through sycamore branches to the town walls and beyond to the ancient earthworks of the uplands. Yet the present merging thus into the past does introduce an element of melancholy here. Certainly Susan is melancholy and the underlining of her pale slightness prepares for her death in the not too distant future.

CHAPTER 14

Summary

Susan settles to a comfortable, if not totally happy, existence, in what will be the declining years of her life. Henchard is consistently kind. Elizabeth-Jane is very happy with their unexpected prosperity and begins to develop as an individual whose personality will have a fundamental influence on the course of the novel. Henchard's dependence on Farfrae for both business and personal company increases. He also becomes increasingly attached to Elizabeth-Jane, wishing that she will adopt his name. Susan's opposition, transmitted to her daughter, causes Henchard to give up the idea. Elizabeth-Jane and Farfrae receive identical invitations to a rendezvous at Durnover granary. The meeting seems to be a hoax and after waiting in the rain they leave.

Commentary

As Susan begins to fade into the background, suggesting that her part in the novel is almost done, Elizabeth-Jane is brought by Hardy into the limelight and, in the space of a paragraph or two, developed into a fully-rounded character who begins to have an increasing influence on others, particularly on Henchard. Without ostentation, she emerges as a potentially beautiful, very sensible young woman, enjoying affluence but not taking it for granted. Her dress is detailed. How important is the question of dress in the novel? Little details such as the sunshade suggest that Elizabeth-Jane will keep up appearances in her own modest way. Destiny has brought her comfort and freedom from the constraints of poverty. She is wary of destiny. Incidental references to fate or chance throughout the novel keep in mind the conflict between the part played by external forces upon the action, and the responsibility of the characters for the situations in which they find themselves.

Henchard, captivated by Elizabeth-Jane, does not know how to establish a loving, close contact. He can show a 'tigerish' affection for Farfrae but Elizabeth-Jane can only be in awe of him and his 'leonine' manner. His increasing appreciation of her appearance is only matched by his brusque inability to compliment her upon it, contrasting sadly with the charm of Farfrae. He will give way, a very rare occurrence with Henchard, over the surname question when he senses opposition. He had begun to modify his manner with Farfrae when the latter showed angry reaction. He now fears rebuff from Elizabeth-Jane, evidence of some form of developing sensitivity at least.

Farfrae's precise ledger accounts are already ousting Henchard's vague, age-old practices. Henchard, in leaving more and more of his business to Farfrae, and depending upon him increasingly for male company, is unwittingly inaugurating his own decline. The Scotsman's importance in the plot increases with his contact with Elizabeth-Jane. His approach contrasts with Henchard's. Farfrae is forward but tactful in his blowing away the chaff from her clothes, a slightly ridiculous scene but carried off with aplomb.

While the principal characters interact, the life of Casterbridge, on which all their prosperity depends, goes on.

CHAPTER 15

Summary

Elizabeth-Jane is becoming noticed in Casterbridge and further admired by Farfrae. His friendship with Henchard develops until a head-on confrontation occurs. Abel Whittle, employed by Henchard, is repeatedly late for work and, after warnings, Henchard forces him to work without his breeches. Farfrae counteracts this and he and Henchard clash, Farfrae prevailing. A young boy innocently reveals how much Henchard's stock has sunk, whilst Farfrae's has risen.

Commentary

A pleasant introduction continuing the harmonious development of relationships and the growing appeal of Elizabeth-Jane is followed by the beginning of the break-up in those relationships. It almost seems that as a rest from the turbulent or ever-volatile presence of Henchard, Hardy could with obvious pleasure delineate the continuing development of Elizabeth-Jane. Earlier she is restrained; now she is so feminine that it is almost too much for her.

Henchard's working methods with his men, illustrated graphically in the Whittle saga, emphasise his character traits of impetuosity and explosive irascibility. He hurries Whittle along without thinking, until faced by Farfrae. Farfrae handles the matter very competently; with immediate determination but also understanding, he sees that Henchard has placed himself in a situation he regrets, and he lowers the tension. It is an exercise in management and Farfrae wins a moral victory. Symbolically, a child is introduced to make Henchard aware of Farfrae's ascendancy in the public esteem. The chapter ends on an ambivalent note. Henchard's reactions to Farfrae are by now unpredictable but he is won over once more by the genuine nature of the Scotsman's regard. His moods change from moment to moment yet with a small residue of resentment remaining.

CHAPTER 16

Summary

Henchard is now formally courteous to Farfrae in business matters but the former warm social intimacy is dying. In due course Farfrae leads a group planning a celebration on a day of national rejoicing. Stung to emulation, Henchard plans a similar event. Rain ruins Henchard's programme but Farfrae has protected his from the weather and enjoys a huge success.

Casterbridge dignitaries compare the methods of the two men, suggesting that the manager is better than the master and will replace him. When this is jocularly put to Henchard in Farfrae's presence, Henchard impulsively announces that the Scotsman is leaving his service. Farfrae takes him at his word.

Commentary

Henchard displays another side of his character. He is courteous to Farfrae in a calculating manner. We do not associate 'good breeding' with Henchard. A contrived courtesy is not natural to him for he is not a man who finds it easy to dissemble. Thus his courtesy goes to extremes. This friendship has been precarious from the start, as if forced by Henchard.

By now Farfrae has established a position in the town. He is the leading spirit in the holiday celebration. Ironically it is Henchard, generously lending rick-cloths, who protects Farfrae's celebration, while his own is ruined. Henchard's, in typical Henchard style, was to be a celebration in the grand manner. He places it out of town for he needs the space but his choice of location is a bad one and he had not planned ahead. Farfrae chooses a location in the town, handy for everyone, hangs the rick cloths and creates an intimate community feeling. Farfrae's is a co-operative effort. Henchard's grand gesture will be paid for by himself; he is not mean and the food will be distributed amongst the poor people of the town. It is, however, one grand impulse gone awry. The townsfolk compare methods, and Henchard's are judged primitive.

Farfrae's cleverness in making use of the trees is emphasised. The townspeople admired a novel idea, introduced into an old-fashioned town, by a new-comer. He is popular with the women, as is obvious from the reaction to his uninhibited dancing, and respected for the best of reasons by the men. This is the watershed for Henchard and his decline has begun in this contest, which he impulsively created.

Faced with adverse criticism, Henchard's reaction could not be more extreme. Smiles become antagonistic glares; gloomily he announces Farfrae's dismissal. He cannot stop himself but his gloom suggests a struggle. He goes home but only 'apparently' satisfied, putting on a front. Henchard with a sinking heart is a sad and lonely figure.

CHAPTER 17

Summary

Farfrae deliberately leaves the dancing and walks home with Elizabeth-Jane indicating that he would like to propose to her. He remains much on Elizabeth-Jane's mind. Instead of leaving Casterbridge he buys a small corn business, making a clash with Henchard, though not of his seeking, almost inevitable. His business prospers. Henchard forbids Elizabeth-Jane to see him and writes Farfrae a note brusquely asking him not to see her. His antagonism towards his former friend grows with Farfrae's increasing success.

Commentary

Elizabeth-Jane is lonely, having no-one but her mother in whom she can confide. Farfrae is the only person outside the family circle who has shown anything more than passing interest in her. The story could have developed happily for Elizabeth-Jane had Farfrae and Henchard remained friends; she dreams of marrying Farfrae, her mother desires it. However she must take refuge in make-believe, as with the letter heading and dressing-up, sadly aware that it is but make-believe.

Hardy speculates on Farfrae's business success. If character is fate and Farfrae's success is due to his character, how applicable are the implications for Henchard? Is he doomed by character?

Henchard's extreme reaction to Farfrae's setting up in business is a commercial war. He has no business talent at all for a prolonged campaign but having impulsively joined battle, like a wounded buffalo he will never break off. Again, the irony is that there was room for both Henchard and Farfrae. Henchard creates the dramatic opposition in his own mind and reacts with the grand gesture.

Casterbridge develops before us with the corn-market and its merchants. Business styles reflect the opponents' characters. Farfrae is always busy, mingling with the crowd and seemingly at home and respected. Henchard is increasingly alone, 'cankered in soul'.

CHAPTER 18

Summary

Susan is very ill. Henchard receives a reply to the earlier letter to the woman in Jersey, whose name is Lucetta, asking for the return of her letters to him. She is passing through Casterbridge and suggests a meeting to collect them. She fails to keep the appointment and Henchard returns home with the letters. Susan, weakening fast, leaves a letter for Henchard locked in her desk, not to be read until Elizabeth-Jane's wedding day. She reveals to Elizabeth-Jane that she had brought her and Farfrae together at Durnover Barton, hoping that they would eventually marry. Susan dies and Mother Cuxsom gives a moving commentary on her passing.

Commentary

An important chapter, beginning the development of a dormant element in the plot. As Henchard's wife is dying another woman comes back into his life with a reply to his earlier letter and a proposed meeting. There are obvious parallels with the return of Susan and Elizabeth-Jane into Henchard's life unexpected, from a past regretted but eventually accepted. His relentless sense of justice makes him consider marriage to Lucetta, though he is glad she does not keep the appointment. The letters must contain secrets and their significance must emerge, as will the importance of Susan's letter to her husband, locked away in her desk.

Farfrae is kept in mind. With characteristic delicacy he calls at the house, fulfilling a normal social role. Henchard has little use for the niceties of social behaviour. Details of the death and laying-out procedure are already the subject of gossip around the town pump. Such details become the substance of local legend and the source of its philosophy. The balance is nicely maintained. The genuinely moving reminder of the last desires of the unobtrusive Susan and the epitaph with its sad conclusion and Biblical rhythms is counterbalanced by Longway's justification of Coney's digging up the pennies and the philosophy of the living, 'money is scarce and throats get dry'. Life must go on and money is too important to be wasted in Casterbridge.

Susan has her moment even if it is in death but, as in life, her wishes are only half-considered. The one intention is to be buried in a respectable manner so we are given the details of the traditional apparel, supplementing the details of clothes given in so many other places in the novel.

CHAPTER 19

Summary

In a domestic atmosphere, three weeks after the funeral, Henchard introduces the subject of her father to Elizabeth-Jane. He tells her that he had married Susan when they were young and that he and not Newson was her father. Susan had thought Henchard was dead when she re-married. A bewildered Elizabeth-Jane writes a change of name note for the Caster-bridge Chronicle. Searching for his earlier document, Henchard finds Susan's letter with the seal cracked. He reads it and discovers that Elizabeth-Jane is Newson's daughter after all. Her features when asleep confirm this to Henchard. Acutely miserable, he wanders along the river-bank, deciding finally to keep the truth from her. In the morning, recovered from the initial shock, she cheerfully accepts her new father, to Henchard's great discomfiture.

Commentary

Henchard's isolation is emphasised with his wife dead, Farfrae – still thought of at times as friend and helper – at odds with him, Elizabeth-Jane the only refuge against the 'stolid loneliness' which his life is becoming. He cannot endure her thinking Newson to be her father but must bind her to himself. On tenterhooks, forcefully and yet as tenderly as he can, he claims her as daughter; even his pathos is 'vehement', as, in anguish, he asks why her father should seem so dreadful. The announcement must be made imme-diately, as if Elizabeth-Jane, in writing the note for the newspaper, is renouncing Newson for ever. After the restlessness and the exciting achieve-ment of his aim he is stunned by the news in Susan's letter, as all readers must be also. The surprise and irony are most effective. He wanders in the part of Casterbridge suited to his mood, the cold, dark river bank below the gaol and gallows site. The river paragraph echoes the gloom and turmoil co-existent in Henchard's mind. He wonders if he is being punished by some fate. We are beginning to feel sympathy for this man who so consistently seems to invite unhappiness while desperately wanting close human contact. Her cheerful acceptance of him as father is the final ironic blow! 'Miserable insipidity' sums up the empty pleasure he gets in the realisation of his most treasured project.

CHAPTER 20

Summary

Elizabeth-Jane is increasingly criticised by Henchard for her apparent shortcomings. She is more and more alone, avoided even at mealtimes by Henchard. Visiting her mother's grave, she observes a pretty, well-dressed woman looking at the headstone.

Henchard is soured at not becoming an alderman, particularly as Farfrae has joined the Town Council. A rare inadvertent dialect word from

Elizabeth-Jane prompts him to write to Farfrae inviting him to take up his courtship of the girl. Elizabeth-Jane's evident disillusionment with life draws the attention of the well-dressed young woman who offers her a post as companion-housekeeper in High-Place Hall.

Commentary

Henchard's aversion to Elizabeth-Jane reaches neurotic proportions, compounded of his own bitter sense of loss, a growing conviction that things are going against him and a strong sense that his dignity and social standing have been threatened by Elizabeth-Jane's few and forgivable lapses. He is becoming gloomily introspective, questioning his luck since 'The King's Arms' supper. Everything is exaggerated. Farfrae is now a 'treacherous upstart' but one who can be used to rid Henchard of the encumbrance of Elizabeth-Jane. Farfrae is still interested in her and appears briefly but significantly, following Elizabeth-Jane to the churchyard yet biding his time. He seems less impulsive than hitherto, the business man tempering the romantic. Elizabeth-Jane's outspoken distress leads to contact with the mysterious out-of-town lady, whose carriage and dress seem all freshness and grace. The lady's support of Henchard is more than would be expected of a stranger. The contrast between Elizabeth-Jane and the stranger is marked, with Elizabeth-Jane naively astonished that elegant handwriting is not a pre-requisite for residence at High-Place Hall. There is a suggestion, however, that freshness is more individual than fashion.

CHAPTER 21

Summary

Much impressed by the sophisticated lady, Elizabeth-Jane goes through the dusk to look at High-Place Hall, where the lady appears to be in residence. She leaves by a back door into an alley. Not wishing to be discovered she hides when she hears footsteps. Thus she does not recognise Henchard who goes into the house by this rear entrance. At home she tells Henchard she would like to leave. He agrees and offers her a small annuity. The next day she completes arrangements with the lady, Miss Templeman, and is on the point of leaving when Henchard arrives. Surprised, he asks her to stay but she is set on leaving and gives her address as High-Place Hall. The name has a dramatic effect upon Henchard.

Commentary

Her obsession with the new prospects in her life takes Elizabeth-Jane to the Hall. It overlooks the market place, convenient for observation of individual and social life, yet the back leads on to another Casterbridge. The 'leering mask' looks on to the alley, a watcher of intrigues in the past, perhaps symbolically watching the intrigue developing in the present.

Henchard's blind indifference to Elizabeth-Jane must seem to her another incomprehensible quirk of fate. It is significant that he can make her independent and himself independent of her through a small annuity. Money can still take the place of affection. Yet Henchard's surprise and regret at her rapid departure is genuine. He can change mind and mood in an instant and the look round Elizabeth-Jane's room is sufficient to convince him of her quality. He does, at least, admit that he had spoken roughly to her. Leaving him for the first time, she moves into a central position between the characters; all are gravitating towards High-Place Hall.

CHAPTER 22

Summary

Henchard's reaction is explained by a flashback to the previous night. A letter from Lucetta at High-Place Hall suggests marriage and the lonely Mayor is not unenthusiastic. He shrewdly guesses at the inheritance after an abortive visit. Even for Henchard, money adds charm. Another letter gives details and also comments on Elizabeth-Jane's function, an excuse for Henchard to call. Henchard calls but Lucetta pleads an engagement, suggesting the next day. Henchard excuses her but obstinately decides not to go. The next day Elizabeth-Jane and Lucetta sit watching the market, Lucetta eagerly anticipating Henchard. Henchard does not call and Lucetta's enthusiasm for him is cooling. Suspecting Elizabeth-Jane to be the stumbling block, Lucetta sends her out, writing yet another letter to Henchard. A visitor is announced but it is not Henchard.

Commentary

Lucetta's first letter reveals a mixture of light-heartedness and practical suggestion, with some concern for other people. She is anxious for security and the Mayor will give her an established position in the town. As a first reaction, Henchard's strong sense of duty welcomes marriage, and his loneliness is acute now that friend and family are gone. The second letter gives more details but also shows how Elizabeth-Jane is being manipulated. Henchard's impetuous evening visit underlines the impatient element in his character and the automatic assumption that he will be admitted. The refusal leads to a controlled but irrational decision to go in his own good time, with far-reaching consequences for him. Elizabeth-Jane's unassertive manner and obvious admiration of Lucetta make it easy for her to fall into the supporting role to the mistress of High-Place Hall, at least a more congenial role than that of companion to Henchard. She is impressed by Lucetta's comparative poise and imagined accomplishments, though Hardy's use of the word 'sage' gives Elizabeth-Jane greater weight. Lucetta is lonely in Casterbridge, finds it easy to confide in the sympathetic Elizabeth-Jane, and is impulsively honest in revealing her past. Her less-composed character is evident in the dramatic poses and spontaneous movements, the hysterical sobs and the hiding behind the curtain. The 'flighty' element is still there. Yet she is aware, too, of the need for a permanent companion.

The chapter continues the use of the windows overlooking the market place, convenient for observing the commercial activity of Casterbridge. Farmers and merchants give animation and colour to the background but the emphasis is on money, ruffled cheque books or, more indicative of attitude, ready money.

CHAPTER 23

Summary

Farfrae calls to see Elizabeth-Jane, marriage very much in his mind. Lucetta is attracted by him and holds him in conversation. The conversation is a mixture of the commercial and the romantic, becoming quite intimate as it progresses, against the noise of the Candlemas Fair outside. Farfrae generously hires an old man and his son, thus preventing their separation. He is bowled over by Lucetta, forgetting Elizabeth-Jane and even his business acumen. He leaves with a love affair developing. Almost immediately Henchard calls, brusquely pleading lack of time. He is sent away. Elizabeth-Jane returns and is now seen as a means of keeping Henchard away.

Commentary

The main theme of the chapter is the meeting between Lucetta and Farfrae. Neither expects the other but initial shock is replaced by mutual attraction. This impulsive reaction is in keeping with Lucetta's character. She was half-heartedly anticipating an unromantic Henchard and instead chance sends the man who has charmed all social levels in Casterbridge. Farfrae is described here as nowhere else in the novel; his clothes, his stylish silver-topped switch, are registered immediately by Lucetta to whom such things matter. Their characters are revealed in the conversation. It is inconsequential, each not quite knowing what to say but Lucetta steers it in a personal direction with romantic under-tones. Farfrae moves from money and business maxims to wishing that there were no business in the world. There is just a touch of Henchard in his impulsive change.

The hiring fair is another of the great Casterbridge occasions. It affords an opportunity for a charitable act on Farfrae's part. Would he have done it if Lucetta were not there? The old man is described with great skill. Should we attach a social signifcance to him? He is part of the very busy world observed from High-Place Hall and in the Hall an entranced Farfrae, for the one and only time, forgets a business appointment.

Lucetta has come down in the world and been despised for poverty. Chance has made her rich but experience has kept her from social pretension. She will accept a tradesman. Now that Farfrae has appeared, Elizabeth-Jane is redundant, or, at best, to be used. Fate seems determined to place her in situations where she helps others but where her own happiness seems unimportant. Henchard's arrival, his 'knocks' almost taking the house by storm, comes as an anti-climax. He is brusque with his message and, for once, we do not see him leave. Actions are beginning that he does not dominate, his old flame and his young ex-friend are creating a world from which he is excluded.

CHAPTER 24

Summary

Both Lucetta and Elizabeth-Jane live through the week for Saturday and the market, where they can observe Farfrae, who by now has established himself as a commercial force in Casterbridge. On one particular Saturday a strange machine, which turns out to be a horse-drill, appears in the market place, introduced by Farfrae. Lucetta and Elizabeth-Jane examine the machine which is ridiculed by Henchard. Elizabeth-Jane half-believes she hears Henchard murmur to Lucetta. Farfrae defends his machine with great enthusiasm to the women. Some days later, after seeing Farfrae, Lucetta tells Elizabeth-Jane the story of an anonymous woman and the two men in this woman's life. Elizabeth-Jane is sure that the woman is Lucetta.

Commentary

The chapter is largely concerned with Lucetta and her growing infatuation with Farfrae. He responds whenever they meet, equally infatuated; deferential to Lucetta, he is matter-of-fact to Elizabeth-Jane. She connects with Farfrae in a moment's serious conversation but Lucetta's breaking the reflective spell reduces Farfrae to a young man not quite sure of himself, a mixture of romantic and mercantile impulses.

Earlier, Lucetta had agonised over her London gowns, putting forward the superficial theory that a person becomes the clothes which are worn. Elizabeth-Jane's advice to think less about the problem emphasises the difference between the two women. Clothing is developing into a recurring image in the novel, with all its implications for status and character. Lucetta is now seeing Farfrae alone, leaving Elizabeth-Jane forced to brood on that which can only be painful. Once more it seems her fate to be something of a Cinderella figure by the fireside, approaching happiness but finding that happiness leading only to pain. Lucetta is resplendent in dazzling colour.

Henchard still does business in the market place, Farfrae still being considered an upstart by him. Yet Farfrae is the obvious progressive introducing new methods and machinery. Henchard's comments reveal a closed mind. He can explain the machine but doubts its practicality. Elizabeth-Jane introduces the picturesque image of the sowers. Farfrae, perhaps with some regret, accepts that the old must give way to the new.

Henchard's brief, reproachful aside to Lucetta, his only contact with her since her arrival, contrasts sharply with her rapidly-developing association with Farfrae.

Another aspect of life in Casterbridge is vividly portrayed. Extending the social range, Hardy takes us to the evening market where the labouring classes take over when the merchants and more leisured people leave off. Money dominates every transaction even if it is pence rather than pounds.

CHAPTER 25

Summary

Farfrae calls on Lucetta, almost totally ignoring Elizabeth-Jane. Henchard, too, eventually calls, sees Lucetta alone and offers marriage whenever she wishes. She is evasive, with Henchard gradually realising her reluctance. Both men have forgotten Elizabeth-Jane but she is philosophical about their indifference.

Commentary

Farfrae and Henchard are now direct yet unwitting rivals for Lucetta, but the younger man's looks and personality, together with his shy deference, contrast noticeably with Henchard's proprietory approach and unpredictable changes of mood. But with a rare flash of insight even he realises that his own accent and deportment belong to a more homely Casterbridge than Lucetta's drawing room. His response is sarcasm about her new-found polish and genteel assumptions. Farfrae's passing by in the sunlight while Henchard is doggedly making his point adds further irony.

The meeting leads to Lucetta's passionate determination to have Farfrae. Her money justifies a higher social class but beneath the poise she lacks confidence and wants only security. Farfrae seems to offer love as well. A commercial note is introduced by Henchard's comment of her living on capital – she must be very rich indeed. Her furniture places old-fashioned Casterbridge fifty years behind the times. Civilisation seems to be judged by material objects, property that can be bought and sold.

Elizabeth-Jane is left alone. Her sense of humour helps her together with a balanced view of what life offers and may offer yet.

CHAPTER 26

Summary

Farfrae and Henchard do acknowledge each other in the town and in spite of everything Henchard seeks advice from Farfrae on his matrimonial affairs. The major characters have become inextricably intertwined yet each has only a bare knowledge of the whole situation. Henchard realises Lucetta has another suitor and an ironic meeting at Lucetta's convinces him that it is Farfrae. He determines to ruin him commercially, employing Jopp as his new manager. He plans to use his capital to buy up grain and under-sell Farfrae. The poor June weather suggests a bad harvest and the superstitious Henchard accepts confirmation from a so-called weather prophet that the harvest weather will indeed be unfavourable. He buys in grain in great quantities, gambling on an autumn shortage. The weather changes, bringing a good harvest so that prices fall. Henchard has to sell corn to settle his accounts but can only do so at a loss. He finds himself in major financial difficulties and has to seek the help of the bank. Jopp becomes Henchard's scapegoat and is dismissed, vowing revenge.

Commentary

Henchard, now certain of a rival for Lucetta, must take action. Subconsciously, he may feel that his whole position is being undermined. Though the breaking of the bread-and-butter in Lucetta's drawing room may seem ludicrous, it does bring home that, unlike the bread, Lucetta cannot be shared. Though not sure rationally that Farfrae is his rival he decides impulsively once more and, having decided, will choose the most reckless course of action possible. His judgement is clouded by his desire for revenge. Farfrae, innocently unaware of Henchard's connection with Lucetta, would be happy to end the antagonism.

Henchard seeks out the weather-man in a lonely hamlet; the isolation is strongly emphasised but the matter-of-fact manner and domestic details of the weather-man are underlined too, giving a feeling of mystery yet also of business. He does it for a living.

Elizabeth-Jane's customary acumen makes her point out the folly of Jopp's appointment, but Henchard has made up his mind, and angrily resents her interference. Intent on his plan Henchard becomes hypertense and irrational. The weatherman tells him what he wants to hear. Everything then is on a large scale, the buying, the selling and the eventual mortgage at the bank.

The very basis of Henchard's success and his standing in the community have been compromised. Jopp's dismissal makes a bitter enemy. Farfrae's sympathy is seen to be mockery, Henchard is alone. Elizabeth-Jane remains on the fringe, never considering her own feelings.

The dramatic and social interest in the weather-man scene, beautifully balanced and detailed, reflects Hardy's own interest in folklore. It links up with the theme of the importance of the weather for Casterbridge and its district.

CHAPTER 27

Summary

The weather breaks. Henchard, increasingly a prey to superstition, fears that he is under a curse. Even his waggoner comes off second-best in a Casterbridge encounter. Henchard follows Farfrae and Lucetta to the harvest fields and overhears their lovers' conversation. He confronts Lucetta in her drawing room and by threatening to reveal the details of the Jersey affair, compels her to promise marriage. Elizabeth-Jane is the appalled witness.

Commentary

Farfrae, the outsider, has proved shrewder than all the Casterbridge business men and beaten them at their own game. He is becoming rich and a potential candidate for Mayor. Symbolically, Henchard's load of hay-trusses is toppled over by Farfrae's waggon, though Henchard generously defends Farfrae against his workman's innuendo. Even at this most exasperating moment he retains his old fairness.

Another inevitable rebuff from Lucetta leads to Henchard's following and eavesdropping upon the lovers, thus becoming finally convinced of Lucetta's acceptance of Farfrae. Henchard now acts completely on impulse, dramatically confronting Lucetta. It becomes clear that there was no love, only loneliness and a sense of duty holding Lucetta and Henchard together, dispelled for Lucetta by the conspicuous charms of Farfrae. Henchard, however, driven by jealousy, attacks Lucetta like a prosecuting counsel. The threat to reveal their joint secret is an impulsive one and, had Henchard not been obsessed with his displacement by Farfrae, Lucetta's reaction might have aroused a sympathy which was not lacking in his nature. Lucetta is overwhelmed, fatalistically accepting what seems inevitable. Elizabeth-Jane, compelled to act as witness in every sense, firmly restrains her own emotions.

CHAPTER 28

Summary

The following day, Henchard, sitting as Chairman of Magistrates, has one case to try in Petty Sessions, an old woman accused of being a nuisance. After an almost farcical introduction to the case by the constable, the woman reveals herself as the furmity seller from the fair at Weydon Priors and promptly exposes Henchard's secret. The news spreads quickly and appals Lucetta. Now that she understands all his secret, she cannot face marriage to him. In great distress she decides to go away for a few days to Port Bredy, fifteen miles to the west. Farfrae is also away from home. Henchard is anxious to contact Lucetta. Eventually he hears of her return and of her going for a walk along the Port Bredy road.

Commentary

A short chapter but a most significant one. Henceforward Henchard will decline socially and commercially. The chapter builds dramatically from the semi-recognition of the woman by Henchard, through the near farce of the presentation of the prosecution's case to the abrupt disclosure of the secret. Another ghost from the past appears in Casterbridge. Ironically, this is one of Henchard's finest moments. He makes no attempt at refutation or justification. He is not vindictive, but leaves with dignity, even though he has to run the gauntlet of the dwellers in Mixen Lane, for whom the discomfiture of the great is prime entertainment. Henchard had been a good magistrate. He accepts without question the dictum that he who administers the law cannot be above it. Obviously his first thoughts are of Lucetta, presumably to try to explain.

CHAPTER 29

Summary

Lucetta goes for an afternoon walk towards Port Bredy, apparently hoping to meet someone approaching Casterbridge. Turning back in disappointment towards Casterbridge, she meets Elizabeth-Jane who is anxious about her friend's restless condition. They are chased into an old barn by an escaped bull, which inadvertently traps itself and them inside. They are forced to run frantically up and down to avoid it. In the moment of crisis they are rescued by a man who seizes the lead-staff of the bull with great force and successfully tethers the animal. The man is Henchard, seeking Lucetta. He takes her home while Elizabeth-Jane searches for a lost muff. She is then given a lift in a carriage by Farfrae, returning to Casterbridge from Port Bredy. In discussion with Lucetta, Henchard offers her an indefinite engagement, only asking her to assure his chief creditor that the marriage will eventually take place. Lucetta is now forced to reveal that she had married Farfrae in Port Bredy. The bells ring out in the background and the town band play to celebrate the marriage.

Commentary

Lucetta's unsettledness seems to have reached a new peak, with the details of Henchard's secret moving her to a permanent pitch of restlessness. Even after her holiday in Port Bredy she cannot rest but must walk back towards that town. Hints are given that she expects to meet Farfrae but nothing more. Elizabeth-Jane's generous nature is shown once more by her concern for her friend. The escaped bull wanders into the plot by chance, probably to add an exciting incident to an episode in the serial. It does, however, show Henchard's strength and physical courage. It brings Henchard and Lucetta together, she hysterically grateful, he tender, thinking with gratitude of their association in the past. As if to balance this pair, there are Elizabeth-Jane and Farfrae in his carriage. There are possibilities for changes of alliances. However, any momentary expectation of these meetings providing happiness is dispelled by what is to emerge. The movement of Farfrae's packed boxed indicates something unexpected is to be revealed. Change of circumstances is always matched by change of house.

Ironically, Henchard is at his best when talking to Lucetta, admitting that he had been wrong in forcing her to promise marriage and making for him an uncharacteristic admission that he had been hurt by her questioning his manhood. Henchard here indicates that he had thought at length on what she had said and that she was right. He is man enough to admit this. He also respects Lucetta's feelings. The postponed engagement would give him chance to recover his fortunes. He is not marrying for money – it is Lucetta who brings up the question of helping him financially. Henchard will not accept money from a woman, even Lucetta, whom he regards as his wife-to-be. A number of very positive character traits emerge from this encounter to be overshadowed by the irony of what follows. Henchard's unstable temper is evident again in the face of what he considers unfair prevarication on Lucetta's part. There is more irony to the fact that Mr Grower was Henchard's chief creditor and also witness to the marriage. Henchard's original threat to reveal her secret had driven her, desperate for some brief happiness, into the impulsive marriage with Farfrae, an outcome Henchard could never have envisaged.

CHAPTER 30

Summary

Farfrae joins Lucetta at High-Place Hall. Lucetta is anxious that the unsuspecting Elizabeth-Jane should go on living with them and gradually leads up to the announcement of the wedding. Elizabeth-Jane disapproves strongly, arguing that Lucetta should marry Henchard or remain single. She cannot remain in the house and finds lodgings for herself not far from Henchard's house.

Commentary

Farfrae, always the keen businessman, had remained at Port Bredy to buy corn, Lucetta returning alone. Farfrae's business is obviously flourishing and spreading into the distant countryside. At High-Place Hall Lucetta is in a state of tension – it is doubtful if she will ever attain complete peace of mind. Henchard is now an ogre and Elizabeth-Jane's independence will come as a shock. The latter's sense of rightness demands Lucetta's mar-

riage to Henchard, her mother's experience having deeply affected her
views on marriage. She shows an almost Henchard-like directness and dog-
matism in this conversation with Lucetta. However, her personal control
contrasts directly with Lucetta's outbursts of passion.

CHAPTER 31

Summary

Henchard is ruined, socially by the furmity woman's revelation and
financially by his wild commercial ventures and negligent management.
He is declared bankrupt but behaves with dignity. Public sympathy swings
in his favour but he goes his own way, living in Jopp's cottage, a sad contrast to his former house. Farfrae buys up his business premises and stores.
Elizabeth-Jane tries to contact him but Henchard refuses to see anyone.

Commentary

Henchard's decline is rapid. He seems to lose interest in his business, leaving
it unsupervised and open to malpractice so that his integrity would come
to be doubted. The resultant bankruptcy proceedings take place in 'The
King's Arms', possibly in the same room which had seen Henchard as
Mayor, presiding over the worthies of Casterbridge. Though the situation
is ironic, Henchard emerges impoverished but with enhanced dignity from
this chapter. His offer of the gold watch moves the creditors. Their unani-
mous refusal is a tribute to the presence which he can still command.
Henchard's subsequently selling the watch and giving the proceeds to a
creditor in straitened circumstances says much for his lack of self-interest
and genuine kindness. There is also a determination to have nothing, to
swing from one extreme to the other. It is ironic that the only meticulously
prepared business document Henchard produces in the novel is his debtor's
balance sheet. As Henchard declines, Farfrae flourishes. Henchard's old
business is transformed, muddle giving way to efficiency, exemplified by
the scales and steelyards. In quick succession Farfrae has gained Lucetta
and Henchard's business premises and stores.
  Henchard's self-imposed banishment to a semi-slum on the edge of
Casterbridge marks his isolation from Casterbridge. What are our feelings
concerning this giant in decline? Are we changing our view? As ever,
Elizabeth-Jane tries to help but cannot even make contact.

CHAPTER 32

Summary

The two bridges at the lower part of Casterbridge, are described in detail. Henchard frequents the further bridge where Jopp informs him that Farfrae has bought his old house and furniture. Farfrae invites Henchard to remain in Casterbridge, offering him accomodation in his former house. Henchard refuses and also declines an offer of furniture, but he is grateful.

Elizabeth-Jane works hard to keep herself, and even harder at reading, very much aware of Lucetta and Farfrae in Henchard's old house. Henchard becomes ill and Elizabeth-Jane insists on attending him. Gradually getting better, he abandons the idea of emigration, thinking a great deal on Elizabeth-Jane and his relationship with her. He takes a position as hay-trusser with Farfrae, initially accepting the situation with dogged good grace. However, Farfrae's continued success, which Henchard thinks is at his expense, preys on his mind so that he becomes obsessed with the completion of his vow of temperance and on that date begins drinking heavily.

Commentary

The bridges add to our knowledge of the more sombre side of Casterbridge life. There are failures and even suicides in this community. As with success, misery is graded according to social status. Henchard, though in decline, is still part of the town ritual, seeking the distant bridge, thinking of a new life overseas. Jopp enjoys taunting him on the bridge. In direct contrast is Farfrae's approach soon after with offer of rooms and furniture. Henchard is surprised at something which had cost money being offered free; that is not the commercial ethic. The two men draw together once more, Henchard warming to the other's generosity. Inevitably we look back to their first meeting and wonder at the reversal of roles.

Elizabeth-Jane, as always a willing agent, is instrumental in bringing Henchard back into Casterbridge society. She breaks through his self-willed isolation. Once again there is another person in his life; he is thinking outside himself. He starts as a hay-trusser, not too proud to accept Farfrae's offer. This is the ultimate reversal of roles but he works at first with philosophic determination. Yet his defiantly-unsuitable dress is one indication of how out of place he is. Farfrae remains distant but this tactful behaviour would be misconstrued by a Henchard whose dormant chagrin at Farfrae's success is never far from the surface. Farfrae has Henchard's house, furniture, and proposed wife. The possible election of Farfrae to Mayor is the final blow to Henchard's self-esteem. The vision of an all-dominant Farfrae becomes a fixation and he becomes unbalanced, driven to extremes of hatred, discounting any values or restraints which once might have made him pause. His great moral achievement, the temperance vow, is degraded to nothing as he obsessively awaits the expiration date. We are inevitably reminded of the young Henchard drinking steadily in the furmity tent.

CHAPTER 33

Summary

Henchard begins drinking one Sunday at 'The Three Mariners'. He persuades and then forces the choir to sing part of a particularly vindictive psalm, telling them afterwards that they were singing about Farfrae. Elizabeth-Jane takes Henchard home, apprehensive about his threats against Farfrae. Lucetta meets Henchard who is woundingly sarcastic, causing her to reproach him in a letter which he destroys. Elizabeth-Jane's concern is heightened when she sees the men together in potentially dangerous circumstances. She decides to warn Farfrae.

Commentary

Many chapters of the novel begin with descriptions of life in Casterbridge itself, reinforcing the background against which the action takes place. As a prelude to the drama this chapter begins with an account of Sunday in Casterbridge, with its patterns religiously observed both in and out of church. The familiar class pattern of Casterbridge is illustrated once more with higher and lower churches.

Henchard has reverted to the drunken aggressiveness of twenty-one years ago but is now made more aggressive by the thought of the work and success of those years being cancelled out by the supposed upstart. He terrifies the choir into performing a psalm filled with hate, lapsing abruptly into a quieter but still obsessed mood when it is over. He takes a childish pleasure in having attacked Farfrae with a song. Elizabeth-Jane guides him home, rather like a great child, his mind on one thing only. His sardonic conversation with Lucetta, prolonged deliberately to wound more effectively, indicates a Henchard set on revenge, yet there remains a Henchard who will a little later destroy Lucetta's compromising letter with some gentler feelings. His feelings for Farfrae seem implacable.

CHAPTER 34

Summary

Elizabeth-Jane warns Farfrae of her fears. He is sceptical but remembers the warning. His plan for a seedsman's shop for Henchard is postponed, but he retains a sincere interest in Henchard's welfare. The aggrieved shop-owner tells Henchard that Farfrae had vetoed the scheme, thus provoking Henchard further.

Lucetta, anticipating disturbance, almost persuades her husband to leave Casterbridge but the coincidental death of the incumbent Mayor leads to Farfrae's nomination and acceptance. An apprehensive Lucetta asks Henchard for the return of her letters. He calls to collect them from the safe in his former home, maliciously reading extracts aloud to Farfrae, asking for comments. Farfrae is reminded of Lucetta by the tone of the letters but does not guess the connection. Henchard is unable to complete his revenge by revealing her name.

Commentary

Elizabeth-Jane's depth of character is recognised by Farfrae, a further emphasis on her developing importance in the novel. Farfrae's sense of obligation to Henchard, too, is emphasised; the plan to put Henchard on his feet again is wholly his. It is ironical that out of good intent comes increased enmity; the petty grievance of another man fuels Henchard's jealousy. The relationship between Henchard, Lucetta and Farfrae is also fraught with irony. Farfrae compares Henchard's hatred to feelings result-ing from rivalry in love, apprehending intuitively the truth but failing to make the connection. The position of Mayor proves too strong a temp-tation for the ambitious Farfrae to refuse. The decision can only lead to tension: first, an even more disturbed Lucetta asking for the letters. second, Henchard seeing Farfrae's appointment as the final insult. Again, in the letter-reading scene, Farfrae links Lucetta with the tone of the letters. Henchard, however, cannot descend to the ultimate treachery of revealing Lucetta's name. A finer side of his nature asserts itself even against his fixed intention.

CHAPTER 35

Summary

Lucetta had heard Henchard reading her letters to Farfrae and had been reduced to near-paralysis. The knowledge that the secret had been kept relieves her momentarily but she determines to meet Henchard herself. She writes yet another letter to him, arranging a meeting in the Ring, when she hopes to persuade him to abandon his persecution. Her appearance in the Ring, plainly dressed and suppliant, reminds Henchard dramatically of his meeting with Susan years before. Strangely moved, he promises to restore the letters and keep the secret.

Commentary

For the moment, Lucetta is the driving force in the novel. Her natural impulsiveness and lack of discretion, exaggerated by fear, force her to yet another compromising letter and what would seem to be an ill-considered meeting in the Ring. Yet she must protect her new-found happiness at all costs. The meeting itself is unexpectedly tender, though the ending of the previous chapter points forward to a Henchard who cannot cold-bloodedly seek revenge. He instantly abandons a cynical mood for one of kindness and genuine sympathy. The memory of Susan still has power to move him. Against the odds, Henchard has introduced positive emotions into the Ring, balancing to a certain extent all the negative associations of the place. Lucetta emerges as a passionately honest character, albeit a rather naive one, anxious only to retain Farfrae. A mixture of superiority and warm response, Henchard is affected by Lucetta's earnestness in spite of himself. When he says 'I can keep my word' (p. 324), we believe him. He is rising again from the abyss and making contact with others in a gentler manner. Will his character permit him to maintain this forward progress?

CHAPTER 36

Summary

As she returns, Lucetta is met by Jopp, who asks for a recommendation to her husband. Lucetta, anxious to avoid being missed by Farfrae, is brusque in her refusal. Rather surprisingly, Jopp is willing to take a parcel from Henchard, containing all Lucetta's letters, to her house. Jopp opens the parcel to discover the letters. On the way to deliver it he meets Mother Cuxsom and Nance Mockridge who inveigle him into 'Peter's Finger'.

There Jopp is persuaded to read the letters and Nance Mockridge suggests a skimmington ride. A stranger making for Casterbridge pauses at the inn and contributes a sovereign towards the skimmington ride, unwittingly ensuring that the ride will take place. Jopp subsequently delivers the letters and Lucetta burns them, persuaded at last that her secret is safe.

Commentary

Hardy has brought the novel to a point of reconciliation, with Henchard in control of his emotions and in a generous mood. He does carry out his promise to Lucetta immediately. It seems an unkind twist of fate that because of Henchard's generosity there should begin a series of events that have little to do with reconciliation or harmony. It seems stupidly negligent of Henchard to entrust Jopp with the letters, even though he wants them to get to Lucetta immediately. Then, as a rule-of-thumb man, he had made a bad job of the seal – is there an echo of his opening Susan's letter? With the passage of the letters to Mixen Lane the novel takes on a more sombre tone. Mixen Lane, described at great length both physically and atmospherically, is cloaked in mists and shadows as were the pastimes of its inhabitants. This area, defined in the most extended descriptive passage in the book, establishes an underside to the prosperous surface of Casterbridge.

It seems fitting that the skimmington ride, a mixture of envy, malice and ribald amusement, should emerge from the depths of the Lane. Hardy is drawing on Dorset custom here as he could well have read about a local ride as late as 1884.

The stranger with his two to three weeks' business in Casterbridge adds mystery and another level of interest. In actual fact the plot is being manipulated drastically. For the moment he remains the first new character, wandering in as all the others have done, but with definite business in mind. Described in some detail, but not identified, he will presumably become involved with the major characters.

As Lucetta burns her letters, the skimmington ride goes forward. Her affair with Henchard had been the result of impulsive kindness, but the subtleties and tenderness of such an affair are to be mercilessly ridiculed.

CHAPTER 37

Summary

A royal personage is to halt briefly while passing through Casterbridge. Henchard disturbs the Council Meeting by suggesting that he should walk

with them to meet the visitor. Mayor Farfrae diplomatically points out
that he is not a Councillor. Nevertheless, on the occasion of the visit,
Henchard, shabbily dressed and with a makeshift Union Jack, steps forward
first to shake hands with the royal visitor. Farfrae pulls him back and
peremptorily orders him off. Henchard stiffens, then leaves. The visit then
passes off satisfactorily but there are some acid comments on the
Henchard-Farfrae relationship made to Lucetta by the wives of certain
town dignitaries. At the other end of the social scale the 'locals' discuss
Farfrae and Lucetta freely and irreverently. The skimmington ride is
going ahead but the considerate Longways and Coney will try to mitigate
its consequences.

Commentary

Almost unwittingly, for his request to walk with the Council had been
only 'a passing fancy' (p. 338), Henchard provokes a confrontation
between Mayor and ex-Mayor, from which it emerges quite distinctly who
has the authority and presence. Farfrae handles the scene in the Council
Chamber effectively but the rejection of Henchard's request only leads to
his whim becoming an obsession and promoting the most extreme course
of action. It will be a gesture of defiance, but even Henchard needs the
stimulus of alcohol before he can put it into effect. There is something
pathetic and absurd about him, in his threadbare clothes, once the symbol
of his affluence, with his exeptional rosette and his home-made flag. The
actual confrontation is dramatic, symbolically in the arena before the
Prince. Farfrae, authority facing crisis, is unhesitatingly autocratic as he
and Henchard face each other, all Casterbridge looking on. The physical
contact is important for what it leads to. Henchard overcomes his initial
impulse to resist, then another impulse moves him to leave the scene. We
can only guess at the reasons for this. Is he nonplussed at what has happened? What is the significance of the fierce light in his eyes? Has he ever
carried through an act of revenge to its conclusion?

Lucetta's devotion to Farfrae and his concern for her are brought out,
as is the backbiting which goes on amongst the wives of the wealthy.
Lucetta's impetuous denial that Henchard helped Farfrae springs from
absolute devotion to her husband. It will have repercussions she could
not have foreseen.

CHAPTER 38

Summary

Henchard withdraws to behind the ladies' stand, hardly able to realise what has happened. He thus hears Lucetta deny that he had ever helped Farfrae. This denial added to the memory of Farfrae's actually laying hands upon him makes him almost insanely determined upon revenge. He asks Farfrae to meet him at the corn-stores behind the Scotsman's house. Henchard, with one arm tied, forces Farfrae into a fight, eventually having him completely at his mercy, forty feet above the ground. He cannot kill him but collapses in an agony of remorse. Farfrae is shaken but determined to keep a business appointment at Weatherbury; Henchard is aware of this and anxiously awaits his return to beg his forgiveness. He wanders about the streets and at the stone bridge hears unusual noises coming from the town. He remains indifferent to them.

Commentary

Farfrae's physically manhandling him seems hardly possible to Henchard, and unforgivable in view of their past relationship. Out of pride in her husband, Lucetta unwittingly adds to the threat facing Farfrae. Henchard becomes an automaton in his obsession with revenge. He can think only of the injury he imagined Farfrae had done to him. Farfrae has challenged him physically and he plans in his manic mood a fight to the death. Yet even in this mood, the most extreme so far presented, he retains an almost quixotic sense of fairness. The tying up of one arm is ludicrous but not uncharacteristic. In this highly-charged mood, too, a song can move him deeply and affect his resolution. Yet, having brought himself to this pitch, he must go through with his plan.

Farfrae's trust and willingness to humour Henchard, even after the interruption at the royal visit, are obvious. He remains kindly disposed towards him. The complexities of character belong to Henchard and the mingling of affection and hate, the instinctive sense of justice, the doggedness in what is essentially a bizarre action and the inability to take advantage of a defeated rival, are all dramatically illustrated in this strange wrestling match. Henchard's token victory brings only a swing from desperate self-justification to bitter self-recrimination. A phrase is introduced describing Farfrae's character as 'a curious mixture of romance and thrift' (p. 350), suggesting the balance which Henchard lacked and which he found so appealing. Just as he had sought out Farfrae for revenge, now, appalled at the depths to which he had sunk, and completely isolated, he must seek him again for forgiveness. Is he aware for the first time that he had lost control of himself; does the pathway to self-awareness begin here? He wanders the streets alone, utterly indifferent to everything but re-establishing some kind of rapport with Farfrae.

CHAPTER 39

Summary

In spite of the fight, which was enough to render most men incapable of action, Farfrae decides to keep a business appointment near Budmouth. However, he receives an anonymous note asking him to go to Weatherbury in the other direction from Casterbridge, sent by some of his workmen planning to keep him away from the route of the skimmington ride. Henchard overhears Farfrae tell Whittle of the change in direction. Lucetta happily awaits her husband's return, ignorant of the developments going on outside. The conversation of maidservants watching the approaching procession draws her to the window at the very moment that Elizabeth-Jane appears to distract her. Lucetta insists on watching, realises the implications of the effigies and falls in an epileptic fit. Farfrae is immediately sent for.

The town constables are stirred from their hiding place by Grower, the magistrate. The subsequent official search reveals no evidence at all of any disturbance.

Commentary

The chapter adds to and ends the climax of violence in the novel that has begun in the struggle between Henchard and Farfrae in Chapter 38. The intensity of Henchard's feelings would seem to suggest violence at some point and if he had been a less complex man Farfrae would have died, symbolically falling from the tower of the business fortress he had captured from Henchard. The fight has brought to a head the antagonism between the principal male characters. Farfrae must at least consider some legal action against Henchard. Yet even in his distraught mood it is characteristic of Farfrae to keep a business appointment, though he argues that it will give him time to think. He obviously does not wish to disturb Lucetta, who will suffer an infinitely greater disturbance, but concern for business propriety seems so much part of his nature that he acts almost automatically. The call to Weatherbury will be more convenient because of his other appointment at Mellstock. As the baser elements of the Casterbridge poor prepare the dreadful shock for Lucetta, the better elements, which means in this case those in regular work, have sufficient regard for their employer to ensure that he will miss the procession. Farfrae had won their respect even if previously he had cut their wages. Lucetta had never become an integral member of the community, only a somewhat aloof member of the privileged classes. It is ironic that she has never been happier than immediately before the eruption of the skimmington ride.

The boisterious malice of Casterbridge's lower classes questions all settled authority. The approach of the effigies is effectively built up, as they meander and turn aside, through the excited conversation of the maidservants. This is as good a spectacle as the royal visit. Alone in her room whilst everything is happening outside, Lucetta can listen calmly until the maidservant's description becomes disturbingly and ironically appropriate. The mention of the front seat in the Town Hall brings the devastating revelation. Elizabeth-Jane, who is always at hand in every crisis, can only watch the mounting hysteria and dramatic fall. The scene's tempo is finely controlled, increasing to the fainting and falling, with the mysterious fading away of the skimmington noise as Elizabeth-Jane rings desperately for servants. To underline the cruel irony of the circumstances, even though Farfrae is sent for immediately, the messenger rides in the wrong direction.

The second half of the chapter balances tragedy with comedy, though comedy with disturbing echoes of what has gone before. The law officers are ineffectual in the tradition of Dogberry and Verges, constables in Shakespeare's comedy, *Much Ado About Nothing*. The magistrate is efficient but no match for the practised nonchalance and skilled misrepresentation of the gang from Mixen Lane. The lords of misrule can still create successful chaos in the county town.

CHAPTER 40

Summary

Henchard comes upon the dispersing skimmington ride. Unable to settle, he seeks Elizabeth-Jane at Farfrae's house. He is told of Lucetta's collapse and also that Farfrae was being sought on the Budmouth road. His information that Farfrae had gone to Weatherbury is ignored and Henchard sets out to meet Farfrae himself.

Farfrae suspects treachery from Henchard, refusing to return to Casterbridge immediately, in spite of Henchard's almost desperate pleas. Henchard returns to Casterbridge and talks to Elizabeth-Jane at Farfrae's house. Later, Jopp tells him that a sea-captain has been looking for him. for him.

Farfrae arrives two hours later to spend the last few hours with his
dying wife. Their conversation is not recorded. Henchard spends the night
restlessly enquiring about Lucetta, concerned also for Farfrae and anxious
to see Elizabeth-Jane. He hears of Lucetta's death at dawn.

Commentary

Henchard is increasingly restless and aware of isolation. His obsessive wish
to be near Elizabeth-Jane brings him again to Farfrae's house, the centre
for all those for whom he has shown any affection. Hardy emphasises his
action in pulling the doorbell to indicate an unexpected delicacy in
Henchard, who is genuinely moved when he hears what has happened.
Anxiety for Lucetta and contrition for previous actions impel Henchard to
find Farfrae himself, but contrition becomes despair when Farfrae's sus-
picion of him leads to Henchard's most desperate realisation of what he
has done to their friendship. He can never completely forget that first
close relationship. He has now become aware of himself as others see him.
The short sentences spurt out pleadingly as Henchard runs alongside
Farfrae's gig, once Henchard's own, ending with the unequivocal 'my heart
is true to you still'. Rebuffed, Henchard curses himself, not others, utterly
depressed. He is still careful, however, to make sure that his presence on
the road will not delay Farfrae.

In the depths of his despair he gains some comfort from talking to
Elizabeth-Jane. He responds to the affection she continues to show – he is
desperate for that affection and the old barrier of her parentage seems to
matter less. Her warmth inspires him to plan a future. Ironically, Jopp,
always the bearer of bad tidings, tells him of the sea-captain's visit. His old
self for a moment, Henchard metaphorically closes the door. The sea-
captain, however, will not go away.

Farfrae's remorse at mistrusting Henchard is emphasised, part of the
complex see-saw of emotion between the two men. The account of
Lucetta's last hours includes what amounts to a critical commentary on
Farfrae in Casterbridge. Her death, avoiding histrionics, is indicated by the
symbol of removing the cloth from the knocker.

CHAPTER 41

Summary

Elizabeth-Jane calls at Henchard's cottage confirming the news of Lucetta's
death. She falls asleep while Henchard is happy to get breakfast. He is
taken aback by a visit from Newson, the stranger at 'Peter's Finger'. He is

seeking his daughter but when Henchard impulsively tells him that she is dead he immediately leaves Casterbridge. Henchard, sure that Newson will return and dreading the thought of an empty life ahead, determines to drown himself. However, he sees his effigy floating in the weir pool and takes it for an omen that he should not commit suicide. Anxious about his intentions, Elizabeth-Jane offers to live with him once more.

Commentary

The chapter opens with a gentle and exceptionally considerate Henchard preparing breakfast for the sleeping Elizabeth-Jane and hoping desperately that they could have some kind of future life together. The dramatic re-appearance of her real father, at the very moment when Henchard has come to understand how much Elizabeth-Jane means to him, is shattering. Even as the kettle boils, a symbol of domestic well-being, fate, with pronounced irony, strikes Henchard his hardest blow. The sheer improbability of the encounter, and instant awareness of its consequences, reduces Henchard to a dull echo of his old self. As always in a crisis, he acts on impulse. His lies are completely out of character but he must retain at all costs what seems to him his only possession of any value. Newson's absolute accept-ance of Henchard's story is so incredible that it leaves Henchard in no doubt that he will be back. Henchard takes Elizabeth-Jane's hand with 'anxious proprietorship', a phrase which embodies urgent need to have something to call his own. Ironically, the more Elizabeth-Jane responds to his self-confessed loneliness, the greater Henchard's dejection. The man who has cared little for other peoples' opinions is mortally afraid of his daughter's reaction if the deception emerges. He appreciates only too well the strength of her character.

In his dulled condition he is impervious to the music of the water. The description of the sounds of the water's flow suggests the continuity and variety of nature, but Henchard sees no worthwhile continuity or variety in life. The appearance of the effigy shocks him out of his resolution, bringing home to him the full implications of what he had intended to do. Once more Elizabeth-Jane, whose increasing concern for Henchard's wel-fare adds a further ironic twist, is at hand to confirm and explain. Newson has disappeared in the coach, a man apparently only of comings and goings.

CHAPTER 42

Summary

Elizabeth-Jane and her supposed father begin to establish a settled life together in the seed-shop provided by the Town Council. Farfrae, recovering from Lucetta's death, decides to do nothing about the skimmington ride, for a variety of reasons. Henchard's devoted attention to Elizabeth-Jane is only equalled by his fear that he should lose her. Already Lucetta has become a nostalgic memory for Farfrae. The seed-shop prospers but an expensive muff and many books suggest to Henchard that Elizabeth-Jane is extravagant. He discovers, however, that Elizabeth-Jane and Farfrae are meeting (Farfrae has given her the books) and, not without scruples, spies on their developing relationship. He is bitterly distressed at the possibility of their marriage but resists the temptation to reveal the facts of Elizabeth-Jane's parentage.

Commentary

There is a comparatively settled stage before the drama of the final chapters. Henchard, though gradually losing the fear of Newson's return, struggles with his conscience to justify his action, taking refuge in an ever-increasing devotion to Elizabeth-Jane. The offer of the seed and root business indicates that he still inspires sympathy in the town, particularly from Farfrae, in spite of the fight. Fate, for once, seems to be kind to Henchard; the business prospers and he and Elizabeth-Jane enjoy 'much serenity'. Hardy appropriately places the shop in a 'pleasant, sunny corner of Casterbridge'. The chapter, however, is cleverly mingling the lives of Farfrae, Elizabeth-Jane and Henchard, draws the former two together, leaving Henchard more isolated than ever. Farfrae is cautious in weighing all the characteristics of precipitate action and ultimately does nothing about the skimmington ride, a justified conclusion but approached very rationally. It is in keeping with his character that he should be businesslike, weigh the profit and loss even in bereavement. Henchard would give everything to preserve things as they are. He attempts a subtle delicacy in his relationship with Elizabeth-Jane. His tentative approach, indicated in phrases such as 'garments of humility', 'quite humbly', and 'netted lion' contrasts sharply with his former authoritarian attitude.

Elizabeth-Jane's association with Farfrae destroys the tenuous peace of mind he was developing. Old emotions are aroused; his hatred of Farfrae returns as the Scotsman threatens to take away Elizabeth-Jane. The hatred is fuelled by the realisation that she means so much to him. All his heartsearchings, and it is significant that he now argues with himself rather than rushing impulsively into a situation, hinge on his sense of inevitable loss. He is brought to the point of acting despicably but there is sufficient of the old Henchard still to prevent this.

CHAPTER 43

Summary

Casterbridge takes note of the courtship of Elizabeth-Jane and Farfrae but soon allows it to subside into the accepted pattern of Casterbridge life. Henchard, however, broods obsessively on what he observes, endlessly thinking about his position after any marriage. His course is decided by the re-appearance of Richard Newson. He decides to leave Casterbridge. Elizabeth-Jane, assuming that it is because of her engagement, tries to change his mind, but Henchard is now adamant and she sadly watches him walk out of Casterbridge. She meets Newson at Farfrae's house and in the course of the conversation about the forthcoming wedding Newson casually reveals to her the fact that Henchard had deceived him. She is appalled.

Commentary

The chapter begins with a reminder that life goes on elsewhere in Casterbridge as usual, though there is a great deal of almost commercial interest in Farfrae's future. The phrase 'nineteen superior young ladies' effectively suggests the social aspirations and competitiveness of the more prosperous classes in the town. Significantly, Hardy gives much more attention to the opinions of the patrons of 'The Three Mariners', where Elizabeth-Jane's qualities are recognised.

Henchard alternates between despair and some slight hope. He has become excessively inward-looking yet he is prepared to accept any humiliation provided that he remains in contact with Elizabeth-Jane. Newson's completely unexpected return ends his indecision. In spite of his stepdaughter's obvious sadness, (she is in tears as she tries to persuade him to stay) he must go because he could not bear her reproach. He imagines in detail what would happen and feels already like a man tried and condemned. Yet he takes care not to communicate his distress to Elizabeth-Jane. He leaves Casterbridge as he must have entered it so many years before. Advancing age, which has only brought bitter experience, suggests that there is little hope of a second rise to power for him. At this low ebb in his fortunes he shows something of his old indomitable will, accepting as just whatever miserable consequences there are to his actions, asserting his strength to carry on.

Elizabeth-Jane's grief at his departure is genuine, yet the meeting with Newson is a happy one. She is still very much affected by the parting with Henchard, however, and pays little attention to the matter-of-fact discussion of the wedding. Henchard's absence is felt by everyone in the room to a certain extent; Farfrae is relieved that he has gone, Newson is surprisingly sympathetic towards him, while Elizabeth-Jane can only stare abstractedly through the window. Her mood is dramatically changed by Newson's account of Henchard's deception, even though Newson makes light of the affair. Elizabeth-Jane is adamant, the phrase 'revulsion of feeling' emphasises her shocked rejection of Henchard. The reader thinks inevitably of the lonely Henchard, striding doggedly over Durnover Moor, whilst Newson turns back to the preparations for his daughter's wedding, more concerned with the merrymaking than anything else.

CHAPTER 44

Summary

Henchard makes his way to Weydon Priors and the fairground where he had sold his wife. His continual thoughts of Elizabeth-Jane make him take up his old work as hay-trusser on a farm near the highway from the west. He learns of a wedding and assumes it is that of Elizabeth-Jane. He cuts short much painful argument with himself by impetuously deciding to go, and walks the fifty miles to Casterbridge, pausing only to buy new clothes and a caged goldfinch as a wedding present. He waits outside Casterbridge until the evening, before approaching the wedding reception at Farfrae's house. Sudden lack of confidence makes him enter the house from the back. The sight of Elizabeth-Jane and Newson dancing together is too much for him and he is about to leave when Elizabeth-Jane approaches. She rebuffs his plea for sympathetic consideration and he leaves the house. The birdcage is left in the garden.

Commentary

The chapter is one long, tragic record of Henchard's isolation. He is now a wanderer, largely indifferent to human contact, his most prized possessions some cast-off belongings of Elizabeth-Jane, and, most poignant, a lock of her hair carried carefully in his pocket. He seems impelled to seek out the fair-ground and rehearse again the auction details as if connecting all subsequent events with what he calls his crime. He has become a brooding philosopher, thinking bitterly of the unpredictable nature of life's patterns. These strange patterns produced Elizabeth-Jane, who remains as the one constant factor in his life. The wheel has come full circle, he is once again a hay-trusser, a wanderer looking for work. Yet age and bitter experience have dulled the once vital ambition and there can be no hope of a second rise for him. He rejects himself and the world as worthless but the memory of Elizabeth-Jane keeps some part of him susceptible to gentler emotions.

Much more agonised debate disturbs him before he makes the long pilgrimage to the wedding. His almost pathetic determination not to let Elizabeth-Jane down is shown in his buying new clothes, the best he can afford. We constantly remember the other Henchard in the days of his greatness and fine clothes. His apprehension increases as he approaches Casterbridge. The sound of church bells celebrating the marriage is almost immediately followed by his hearing the wind sighing through the larch trees, a sound much more in tune with Henchard's mood as he stands, with 'bundle and bird-cage . . . a lonely figure on the broad white highway'.

Details such as the washing of his hands in the river and the dusting of his boots emphasise his determination to make as brave a show as possible. The feeble lamps are symbolically suitable for the lowly position in which he sees himself. There are echoes of the days which marked the beginning of Henchard's decline as Farfrae is heard singing with as much vigour as he had done in 'The Three Mariners' years before. The splendid nature of the wedding reception makes Henchard's carefully but poorly-dressed presence seem totally out of place. Instead of walking boldly through the front door, as he had so often done as master and mayor, he goes quickly round the back, glad to seek help from the housekeeper. In his own mind he is no more now than 'a humble old friend'.

The dance again emphasises Henchard's isolation. He is an outsider, seeing only glimpses of the gaiety within. Gaiety has gone from Henchard's life and he is surprised that anyone can enter marriage with such flippancy. Perhaps bemused, he sits and tries to understand. Low in spirits as he is, he reaches a tolerant conclusion. As he thinks, the main characters in his life pass before him, Farfrae rotating as gaily as ever, Elizabeth-Jane still not sure that the pleasure can last, and ultimately Newson, all uninhibited happiness. It is Newson's assured place in the circle that completely unsettles Henchard. His sense of guilt becomes overpowering and he stands, disturbed and indecisive, but strangely impelled to retreat. Chance ends the dance at this moment and brings Elizabeth-Jane to him. Her formal greeting emphasises the distance that is now between them. This is the last, mortal blow for Henchard. The once-proud autocrat anxiously seizes the hand that he had once taken as proprietor and pleads for recognition. Then follows a tragedy of separation. Elizabeth-Jane's first reaction is to reproach Henchard. He has offended against her strict moral code. Her tone is bitter but there is grief in it too and had Henchard renewed his pleading she could well have softened toward him. He, however, cares too little for himself now to put forward reasons for sympathy or excuse. He had disturbed her; with something of his old independence and impulsiveness he accepts responsibility for the distressing situation and makes his decision to leave, this time for good. 'Good-night' becomes 'Good-bye'!

CHAPTER 45

Summary

Elizabeth-Jane and Farfrae settle to normal married life in Casterbridge. Elizabeth-Jane discovers the dead goldfinch. Several weeks later she is told who had left it and she immediately assumes that it was a gift and an indication of his remorse. She begins to feel sorry for the man and Farfrae agrees to her plea for help in finding Henchard. They hear a report of his walking eastward which leads them across Egdon Heath into remote places. They are about to give up when they see Abel Whittle who leads them to a derelict cottage. At the door of the cottage he tells them that Henchard had died half-an-hour previously. In a moving speech, Whittle tells of his devotion to Henchard. He produces Henchard's bitter will with its peremptory commands. Elizabeth-Jane sees that the wishes are carried out. She regrets the unhappy, last parting from him for a long time but lives to achieve a very happy married life in Casterbridge.

Commentary

The final chapter is, of course, dominated by Whittle's account of his accompanying Henchard, by the latter's death and by the production of the will. The presence of Henchard is dominant throughout.

The bird-cage, forgotten or abandoned by Henchard, becomes to Elizabeth-Jane a symbol of Henchard's good intentions. She realises that he was a man caged by his own regrets and remorse, unable or unwilling to excuse himself in the least. Though the song of the bird is stilled, Henchard's present achieves its aim rather more than he had expected. Secure in her marriage, she is anxious to assist the Henchard for whom she now feels pity – a reversal of the roles in the earlier stage of the story, when she walked into Casterbridge. Farfrae's good nature is emphasised here; he is willing to help a former friend in spite of what had happened.

The search develops into a crusade for Elizabeth-Jane, depicted by Hardy with great effect at comparatively short length. She is desperate to instal him in a place where she hopes he could be at peace with himself; she is aware intuitively into what depths of degradation and self-abasement he might deliberately plunge. Casterbridge, with its safe homes, seems far away; the moorland, with its sparse trees, lies ahead. The search is made more vivid by details such as the initial sighting of Henchard. Elizabeth-Jane is in thick, flat fur, indicative of her rise in the world. She can afford now to look after her stepfather. There is haste across Egdon Heath, search near Anglebury, but they lose the track. Farfrae's concern for money emerges and his worry over the cost of accommodation might be criticised as heartless. It must be said, however, that the search seems hopeless.

Chance takes a hand once more and Hardy achieves perhaps the greatest but most effective surprise in the novel. In the midst of the 'wide country', from out of the blasted clump of firs, emerges the shambling figure of Abel Whittle, who has never disappeared completely from the story but who would seem to have little part here. Elizabeth-Jane recognises him as 'poor Whittle', while Farfrae remembers the money he owes Whittle, the first association to come into his mind.

This is a prelude to the cottage, the last building to be described in a novel where buildings seem almost as important as human beings. The cottage is in stark contrast to anything found in Henchard's Casterbridge. It is boarded up and recognised as unfit for human habitation. We are not allowed into the cottage. Henchard's spirit has vanished from the face of the earth and his body in decay must remain sacrosanct. Only the simple, who accept Fate implicitly, can attend it with unquestioning and unstinted devotion.

Whittle's account of the death of Henchard can lay claim to be the most moving passage in all Hardy's fiction. It is an elegy to Henchard, whom he remembers for kindness and who must be repaid with kindness. The man of little intellect who has nothing – he must tell the time by the sun – has the last word on the man who once had everything in this little world. The discreet use of dialect gives the passage authenticity. The rhythm of the sentences gives an inevitable movement towards the end, checked by the sharp reported commands of Henchard but helped on by the persistent going forward of Whittle after each stop. Eventually Henchard seems either glad to have him there, or disinclined to care. Whittle sees that he is low, and 'wambles', and follows instinctively to do him a kindness. It is ironic that Henchard, for all that he once was, should die attended only by a minor character, the least endowed of any in the book. Yet Whittle achieves dignity because he is uncomplicated and strong in a natural sympathy, not easily diverted and seeking nothing for itself.

Farfrae's amazement is summed up in a cliché that perhaps demonstrates that he could not understand how a man could bring himself to such a pass. He had not, of course, been present at the last meeting of Henchard and Elizabeth-Jane. She is shocked to silence and it is not difficult to guess her thoughts.

The final contact with Henchard is through his will – a will that makes a mockery of normal wills of solid Casterbridge citizens. Henchard has nothing to leave save defiant, negative instructions which demonstrate how valueless he had come to regard himself and the customs of his community. His first and only charitable thought is for Elizabeth-Jane. His consideration for her is thrown into sharp relief by his hatred of himself. The remaining six brutally explicit commands would remove all trace of Henchard and his memory from the face of the earth. The spelling mistakes give the document more humanity; they do not detract from its force.

Elizabeth-Jane ends the chapter and the book. Farfrae automatically asks Elizabeth-Jane for a decision. She cannot bear the thought that she had been so uncharitable; Whittle's example must have struck home. She weeps bitterly but acknowledges the fact that it cannot be changed. This was Henchard's destiny. The integrity of the man would be matched by the integrity of the funeral, true to his wishes.

The final paragraphs belong completely to Elizabeth-Jane. She had been a ready and sympathetic helpmate to others all through the novel and she lives to lead others towards a happier acceptance of their particular lot in life. Unlike Henchard, she maintained a balance and was a force for balance in the world. She did not take her own good fortune for granted because after an unhappy youth she had half-expected a painful maturity to be the inevitable consequence. She is amazed at the unpredictability of life's patterns and the unfairness, but she has achieved a wise and enviable stability. Here, too, she seems to speak for Thomas Hardy himself.

4 THEMES AND ISSUES

The Mayor of Casterbridge is set in agricultural England in the first half of the nineteenth century. This does not mean, however, that it is a comfortably rural novel with no relevance for contemporary readers and issues. Put simply, it is concerned with the life of one man, part of, and yet tragically isolated from, the community in which he lives. Other characters, social pressures and the necessity for balance are part of his story.

4.1 THE INDIVIDUAL

Title and sub-title give us the main theme, the life and death of one man within the community in which he established himself. An exceptional man, he became the most prominent citizen of that community, a 'man of character', though not just the good 'character' which the phrase usually implies. This character is not conventional, his good and bad facets combine in a complex and powerfully dramatic presentation of a human being. He is not initially portrayed as an attractive character. His life is not the story of someone with 'sound parish views' (to quote Hardy's poem 'The Conformers'), his death not the occasion of praise from the community which had elected him Mayor. Instead, the end of the Mayor is a tragedy of self-willed loneliness, poverty and rejection of life itself. The depth and power of Hardy's creation involves us with Henchard, almost against our will. He walks into the novel, 'a measured, springless walk, . . . showing a dogged and cynical indifference personal to himself', and we are intrigued but repelled by his drunken rejection of the closest family ties. He walks out to die 'low and faltering' (p. 284), and we experience an enormous sense of loss. Is it too much to claim that our capacity to understand human beings is enlarged and our compassion for their despair broadened by the life and death of Henchard?

Our awareness of and sympathy for the man develop as his understanding of himself and his situation matures and intensifies. We see him first aloof and disgruntled. He has presence and determination in abundance. He is ambitious, skilled in the fodder business and aware that he could be something more than he is. Greatness, however, is couched in terms of money – his immediate aim seems to be one thousand pounds. Marriage has prevented this. Marriage is a fundamental issue in the novel as the basis of family and thus social life. It should spring from attraction and stimulate love and stability in the community. How uncertain is the issue, however? Henchard despises his wife! From the novel's beginning Hardy is examining the ironies of this most binding yet fragile ceremony. Two individuals become one, determined on ideal harmony. Henchard marries Susan at nineteen and spends two years regretting it. Initial expectancy has become brooding resignation, declining to unexciting familiarity, and, worse, resentment that his advancement has been jeopardised.

A psychologically complex character is emerging. Henchard's resentment has become an obsession. Why he married Susan is unexplained. Was it an impulsive yielding to an attraction of opposites? His aggressive temperament now depises her meekness. This tendency to aggression is never far below the dogged determination and apparent indifference on the surface. Some critics see Henchard as an archetypal example of an aggressive personality as studied and defined clinically by twentieth-century psychologists in the wake of Freud's initial research. The imaginative depiction of a psychologically-disturbed Henchard is explored very fully by Rosemary Sumner (see Suggestions for Further Reading), who emphasises Hardy's outstanding grasp of the complexity of human personality and its reactions under pressure. His imaginative portrayal of Henchard anticipates modern scientific research and is endorsed by it. A feature of the aggressive personality is a swing in mood from one extreme to another; a fundamental lack of balance may indicate feelings of insecurity, hardly recognised but compensated for by the necessity to dominate. The selling of Susan shows Henchard at his most aggressive and least attractive. The aftermath of the auction reveals a swing to the other extreme. He despises himself, aware of what he has done, aware of the part played by drink in his losing control of himself and determined not to allow that to happen again. Genuine remorse makes him seek the vanished family. Ironically, he has achieved the state he wished for, but now regrets. His innate sense of justice perhaps acts as a spur to his subsequent achievement. He can only do penance by achieving a rare success, from the extreme of only fifteen shillings in his pocket to the munificence of the Casterbridge potentate.

It is a lonely success, however, and isolation is a fundamental part of it. Bouts of great energy have carried him to the top, but it is unthinking energy, unaware of its alienating qualities. Others sense and reject the implicit aggression. Henchard frightens people away. The Casterbridge business community is content to allow him to get things done, but socially he remains an outsider, even though he is 'the powerfullest member of the Town Council, and quite a principal man in the country round besides' (p. 53). He has not achieved a balance in his life. He remains unpredictable even though always trying to keep himself under control.

We meet him for the second time at the pinnacle of his career but also when things have begun to go wrong. How much chance or good luck has played in his success is unknown. We can assume that Henchard acted on impulse and obviously fortune was with him. Or that he had worked heroically, having few other distractions, at what he knew – the fodder business. He had eventually, however, ventured into new areas and luck seemed to have been against him. It is noticeable that such unreliable speculations are to be no part of Farfrae's success.

Henchard as a poor man had failed to establish happy relationships. Wealth will enable him to try again, to make amends and also aim at a genuine friendship with another man. The chance return of the supposed abandoned family and coincidental arrival of Farfrae find him in splendid isolation, and underline his loneliness. Yet the individual can now make contact with society in the most promising circumstances, through domestic family happiness and the friendship of a charming man. Even so, given the opportunity, Henchard fails again. He is impeccably correct in his attention to the family but unable to express the emotion which his first meeting with Elizabeth-Jane inspired. He forces the pace with Farfrae and only the young man's inexperience and astonishment at his good fortune makes the early relationship of the two men possible. As it is there is obvious disagreement to come, Farfrae being everything that Henchard is not. He has his own determination and is undemonstrative but level-headed in business. His business and social successes are a commentary on Henchard's failures. Henchard affronted means Henchard an enemy but here we begin to appreciate the complexity of his character. He is not a natural enemy. He is an individual inept at personal relationships, but there are flashes of tact, delicacy and generosity that are not out of place or artificial, even if they are overwhelmed by anger, jealousy and a dislike of losing. The inter-relationships of Henchard with Farfrae and with Lucetta are a disaster and he does his best to destroy the one loyalty that remains constant, that of Elizabeth-Jane. He fails as family man and friend, and deliberately sets himself apart from society.

It is as if he had to sink to a situation in which he had lost all the trappings of worldly success before he becomes aware of something outside himself, a desirable quality that is not money or property. This he recognises in the unselfish quality of Elizabeth-Jane. There is hope for this individual to re-establish himself in the community; those who know him best want this for him. The vestiges of the old aggression battle with this new regeneration through love. Chance brings Newson back and Henchard commits his crime, this time against himself and against society; he lies to retain his one contact with warmth and stability. He leaves Casterbridge to avoid the disintegration of that fragile stability he had achieved. His final return is motivated by love and a wish to be accepted. The one lapse in immediate understanding on Elizabeth-Jane's part is enough to ensure the final departure. The individual Henchard still retains some pride and dignity and leaves as determined as he had come only to falter and reject society for ever. Ultimately he has turned his aggression upon himself.

4.2 RETRIBUTION AND FATE

His lonely death can be seen as terrible retribution for Henchard's initial sin. He had broken the social law, shrugging off his social responsibilities and condemning those to whom he owed the greatest affection to a fate to which he seemed indifferent. That this should have enabled him to prosper is ironical; that the agent of his downfall who reveals the skeleton in the cupboard should be the old furmity woman, herself very much declined in the world, seems the supreme irony of fate. The part played by chance and fate or destiny in the novel is an important theme. Chance implies randomness or an ordering of events over which man has no control and therefore no means of averting. It plays an integral part in everyone's life; supersitition is a vain attempt to assert human supremacy over it. Henchard was superstitious to no avail. As narrator, however, Hardy introduced the statement that 'Character is Fate' (p. 114). If this were so then what happened to Henchard was inevitable, his particular aggressive character determined his dramatic rise and self-ordained fall. Apart from minor adjustments there was little he could do to avert his fate.

As with many such statements, 'Character is Fate' has one truth in it. But it diminishes Henchard. He does not seem to us the victim of a malignant or even indifferent Fate. He is certainly not a malignant character; he is an exceptional character but not an abnormal one in the psychiatric sense. He is exceptional because his personality is one of extremes, giving him the capability for great good or great evil. He is the victim of his moods but the impulsive extreme action is always followed immediately by self-realisation and remorse. There is a capability for growing self-awareness and awareness of the needs of other people. He suffers, and becomes a more benevolent person because of it. How far personality, how far circumstances, how far pure accident are responsible for his rise and fall is a fascinating question. Being Henchard, his character ensures that everything will be on no mean scale.

The Henchards of this world are difficult people to live with and the main theme of the novel is the life of an exasperating, volatile individual for whom few people have any real affection, and who seems his own worst enemy.

Yet he retains his own integrity and it is an essentially human person who deliberately turns his back on the world when the one person who had offered him an insight into a life of quiet harmony momentarily fails him. Perhaps there was no place for him in Casterbridge but his passing seems to leave lesser men behind. (Further discussion of Henchard will be found in the Character section.)

4.3 THE COMMUNITY

The major characters in the novel are searching for stability within their environment: Susan seeks to re-establish a legal relationship, Elizabeth-Jane wishes to improve her education and enjoy a settled position in the community, hoping against hope that her early ill-fortune may eventually be tempered by happiness. The theme of compassionate understanding. unselfishly displayed, is her contribution to the novel. Lucetta, in contrast, lives on the surface of things, demanding more from the community than she can return. Farfrae seeks a base from which to further a career. Stability for him is success. Casterbridge offers the environment and opportunities. Here they all contact Henchard who offers security on generous terms in return for complete involvement with him emotionally.

In fact, as the stability of the community depends on commerce, so does that of the individual. Henchard is buying human companionship just as he sold companionship at the auction. His final rejection of aggressive competition is the ultimate theme but nowhere else in Hardy's novels is there such a commercial atmosphere, so much emphasis on buying and selling. The market-place is the centre of Casterbridge, time and again the reader observes the bargaining at all levels. Pounds, pence, cheque books, overdrafts, creditors, bankruptcy, wages, employers and employees are all significant. From barns full of corn to shop windows full of implements and work clothing the basis of the commercial bustle is emphasised. The theme expands to include the overwhelming importance of the weather to the economy, introducing age-old belief in superstition as a means to commercial success. Already, however, such beliefs belong to the past, sought out self-consciously down secluded paths. The new commerce is forward-looking and the clash between the old and the new adds another dimension to the novel. It is also a clash between generations, young and old, between practices which promise more efficiency and profit, intro-duced from outside the community, and established patterns. Time-honoured methods of cultivation will be challenged by machines. Even the entertainment of Weydon Priors Fair becomes mechanical! Science can improve wheat which once had to be abandoned. Literacy and chemistry are necessary for a successful corn-factor; steel-yard and scale will supersede guesswork and rule of thumb. Business is becoming a matter of accurate bookkeeping and forward planning. The old method (p. 95) disappeared. Henchard and Farfrae are symbolic of this opposition. Henchard is a dinosaur in the modern commercial forest. All kinds of external pressures, national and international, mean that the old agricultural patterns will no longer maintain the community. Casterbridge will adapt as it always has but there will be individual casualties as the young grasp the mantles of the old. Symbolically, Henchard's wagon meets Farfrae's in the narrow street and is overturned. Hardy recognises the practicality and the inevitability of the process, though life and colour may disappear from the High Street. The old must yield to the new.

In many ancient myths there is a ritual sacrifice of the corn-king; the old leader must die so that the crops may flourish in the coming season and the community remain stable. Henchard is a dramatic sacrifice to progress, Farfrae the new dynamic head of business and Council affairs, the organising magician whose community festivals do not go sour. In his turn Farfrae will be succeeded by another Mayor but one developing Farfrae's principles for there is no going back. There is a comparison, too, with the Biblical story of Saul and David. Saul was an energetic and successful leader in the national wars against the Philistines. He fostered David as a son but when the latter's superior organising ability and statesmanship exposed Saul's weaknesses then the jealous Saul, suffering from melancholia, planned to kill David. There is always potential tragedy in a period of transition.

Other issues emerge as we become more familiar with Casterbridge. Hardy takes us along the streets but also along the lanes and back alleys. The rear of High Place Hall belies the proud decoration of the front. The structure of Casterbridge society, with its opposites, becomes a theme, the relationship between rich and poor an issue. There is constant emphasis on buildings in Casterbridge, from the luxury of the Hall, through the solid respectability of Henchard's former house (the furniture is also significant), to the drab darkness of Mixen Lane and 'Peter's Finger'. Public places of entertainment are stratified, from 'Peter's Finger' rising to 'The Three Mariners' and beyond to 'The King's Arms'. Even the churches cater for different levels of society (p. 206), the length of sermon denoting the quality of the congregation – possibly a mixed blessing. The most extended description in the novel is that of Mixen Lane. The wealthy Casterbridge community is relatively close to those who do not share in its prosperity. Normally they exist in an uneasy harmony but there is always a threat to stability with the emergence of the disgruntled from the slums, threatening the well-being of the greatest in the town riot. At such times law and order seem ineffectual; there is a very inadequate police force in Casterbridge!

Change will bring new problems to a community which traces its ancestry back to ancient Rome and has even older settlements on its boundaries. A Mayor such as Farfrae can be relied upon to promote change and efficiency for the good of the community. The basic issues remain the same, however. Work and its commerce hold the society together, involving the ebb and flow of human relationships as human beings rise and fall in competition with each other, and, more particularly, the search for harmony within the community of the individual personality. All Casterbridge's long line of Mayors, not least Farfrae, would contribute to these issues from their position of high authority. Henchard, however, was a Mayor of singular character. His rise and fall is the stuff of legend!

5 TECHNICAL FEATURES

5.1 THE PLOT

The novel was begun in 1884 and almost completed by early 1885. As serial publication was to begin in The *Graphic* in January 1886, Hardy revised his original extensively to get an incident into every part. He later maintained that he had damaged the plot as an artistic whole more recklessly than perhaps any other of his novels. He revised the serial again for book publication, removing some cliff-hanging endings involving accidental encounters, including, for example, one where Farfrae fails to recognise Lucetta when with Henchard. In the 1886 serial, Henchard, believing Susan to be dead, married Lucetta because of what she had done for him. In the 1895 edition he has reverted to his original intention of an illicit relationship. In spite of his qualification and revisions, however, Hardy believed that the plot was quite coherent and organic.

These are apt adjectives, even if the growth does seem forced at times. There is a feeling of cohesion and inevitability about the novel's construction that recalls the structure of classical Greek tragedy. The unities of place and action are observed within the wider framework of a novel and, if the first two chapters are accepted as a Prologue, then the time sequence is concentrated enough to maintain the powerful impetus of the book. Henchard walks on to the stage of the novel and, with an impulsive act repudiating the family and social order, sets in train a sequence of events that will end with his walking off to die.

The plot then develops interaction with a small group of characters whom Henchard at first dominates but who successively escape that domination, leaving him isolated and poignantly aware of a world in which there is no place for him. Yet he does loom over that world and the plot has the other characters carrying on their activities in a manner that seems almost inconsequential. The great scenes of the novel – Henchard and the auction; in 'The King's Arms'; in court with the furmity woman; at the soothsayer's; the fight; Henchard running beside Farfrae's gig; Henchard outside the wedding celebrations; these and several others remain longest in the memory.

The plot, it must be admitted, does creak from time to time. The appearance, and re-appearance of characters, especially the casual wanderings of Newson, sometimes seem arbitrary rather than inevitable. But this does not affect the strength of the overall structure, hinging on Henchard himself, which has a dramatic sweep and unity which totally convinces. Henchard rises and falls in an accelerating pattern, his hopes sustained and dashed until the bitter end. As he falls, Farfrae rises; Elizabeth-Jane rises also to achieve a balanced happiness. Through this structuring Hardy changes our attitude to Henchard. As the novel progresses we move from antipathy to complete involvement with him, and belief in him. Hardy anticipated and disarmed criticism with his own comment on the novel. He wrote, 'I fear it will not be as good as I meant, but, after all, it is not improbabilities of incident but improbabilities of character that matter'.

Any consideration of the plot must include Casterbridge itself. The town becomes much more than background to the action. The description of its structure and life are so realistic that the realism rubs off on to the characters and gives them an extra authenticity. The town is presented, too, as a comment on the action. Casterbridge has seen many men come and go, their strangeness and motivation long since forgotten.

Hardy was aware of some weakness of plot. He was also aware that he had achieved a total effect that transcended any such weakness. His characters are consistently true to themselves, the lesser ones revolving round a giant whose every action captures the imagination and who convinces us that he can act in no other way.

5.2 STYLE AND LANGUAGE

The entry of Susan and Elizabeth-Jane into Casterbridge, in Chapter Four, illustrates Hardy's varied use of language and stylistic devices. The initial effects are essentially visual. Anticipating what would become a favourite practice of the cinema director, he first gives us a distant shot, afterwards zooming in on the detail. Casterbridge is seen from a hill outside. We are expectant observers who approach, pause for a moment, then look in to share whatever is going on inside. This taking of the reader into town, inn or individual room gives a sense of familiarity and close involvement; it is a recurring practice throughout the novel.

Casterbridge in the setting sun takes on the romance of a promised land of towers, gables and casements (p. 47). It is necessary first to go through a dark tunnel before emerging into a cosy lamplight, giving a physical sense of warmth and comfort. The sense of an enclosed, secure community is reinforced by the sound and rhythm of the words Hardy uses, as in the tight and alliterative, 'within the walls were packed the abodes of the burghers' (p. 63).

Once inside there is a general impression of housefronts and roofs, old and haphazard, before the detailed catalogue of shop-windows. This has a cumulative rhythmic effect, item succeeding item in a headlong manner, suggesting, by its sound and complexity, a busy working community that has everything it needs. This list technique is used elsewhere as in the paragraph of sports activities planned for Henchard's celebration, the leisure counterpart of this working list.

Hardy's method is to suggest a building rather than describe it in full, giving details as we would normally gather them in passing, before taking us inside. As we continue the walk down the High Street, the creeping plants on the church stonework lead the eyes upwards to the battlements; 'grizzled' and 'massive square' establish the strong and ancient presence of the church in the twilight. Hardy employs sound to announce the end of another, ordered Casterbridge day. The church bell begins rhythmically:

'a bell began to toll with a peremptory clang'

Many of Hardy's phrases and even sentences can be scanned as poetry. The clatter of shutters and chiming of clocks is part of the pattern built up, part of the rhythm of Casterbridge life. Then the tallcase clocks, described in an unusually long simile for this novel (p. 48), and the unsynchronised chiming, add a quaint element to the scene. Abruptly, Hardy changes the tone, as he will do frequently, and presents us with a belligerent Nance Mockridge and unprincipled bread.

The 'looking-in' procedure is used with the three hostelries. We gaze into 'The King's Arms' with its 'spacious bow-window' and 'main portico' at our first public event, the mayoral banquet. 'Pantomimic laughter' and 'convulsive grimace' give the flavour of the after-dinner spectacle (p. 55). A little later we look in on a more private gathering. 'The Three Mariners' is conjured up by its stone windows, tightly-shuttered, and its almost anonymous sign. Its entrance is narrow and long, as are the entrances of many buildings in Casterbridge. Once inside, however, we are made to feel at home through the use of domestic detail. The atmosphere created here is harmonious and Hardy adds to it with Farfrae's singing, effectively contrasting with the behaviour of the Mayor's banquet. The scene also introduces at length a different kind of language, slow, anecdotal, shrewdly philosophical in a homespun manner, the language of the country, so detested by Henchard as indicating the lowest social status. Hardy's dialect has been criticised as artificial but, once accepted that a strictly accurate rendering of a dialect is likely to be unintelligible to most readers, then Hardy's modification of Victorian Dorset colloquial speech has an authenticity and rhythm that convinces.

To complete his pattern of stratified places of entertainment, Hardy takes us, in due course, on another tour to lesser Casterbridge, its thoroughfare, Mixen Lane, and its inn, 'St Peter's Finger'. Access here is narrowest of all: its atmosphere is conspiratorial', the language is of crime and disaffection; its 'guests' grow 'boisterous' and there are cudgels in the chimney.

There are other visits and observations in Casterbridge. Elizabeth-Jane makes her way to Henchard's house and is welcomed amid his very heavy furniture, eminently suitable for an over-bearing personality (p. 77). Hardy also uses the device of someone looking out of a house, framed by the window. Elizabeth-Jane watches Henchard and Farfrae (p. 100), Elizabeth-Jane and Lucetta gaze at the market place from High-Place Hall, enjoying a panoramic view of Casterbridge movement and colour (p. 160), while the isolated Elizabeth-Jane looks from her small lodgings at Farfrae and Lucetta in Henchard's old home. The longest visit is made by Henchard when he penetrates deep into the countryside via turn-pike road, lane, cart-track, bridle-path, footway and hindering brambles until he arrives at the fastness of the weather-prophet's hut. Yet the most poignant visit and observation is reserved for the end, when Henchard looks through a half-opened door to catch glimpses of the most lively and self-engrossed spectacle of all, Elizabeth-Jane's wedding dance. This time we are not taken in but remain outside with him.

Just as dialect is an indication of class, so Hardy makes use of dress as a symbol of rising and falling in the world. We first see Henchard, not ill-clad and with some pretence to style, in a newish coat and waistcoat with white horn buttons. Nineteen years later he is in an evening suit. He hasn't kept up with the style for his suit is old-fashioned, but jewelled studs and heavy gold chain define his status. Throughout, his dress illustrates his fortunes, with the incongruity and associations of the rusty silk hat, gentleman's old blue suit and soiled and shabby, satin stock a sad commentary on the young man whose neckerchief was like a flower-garden (p. 203). This same Chapter Thirty-two has Elizabeth-Jane putting away 'the silk attire of her palmy days' as she settles into her small lodging. Her dress has progressed from plain mourning clothes to increasingly stylish clothing and then returned to the plainly practical, reflecting her indeterminate status. Lucetta, of course, is all money and flamboyance in clothes and movement, though she will tone down her dress when it is necessary to create an effect.

Hardy rarely uses descriptive passages purely for their own sake in the novel. The panorama that Henchard sees when he wakes after the auction (p. 37) takes the eye to the prehistoric fort. The often-quoted passages from Chapter Eleven emphasise the Roman aspect of Casterbridge and the traditions linking this part of the Casterbridge landscape with the present. The paragraph beginning Chapter Thirteen joins sunset, sycamore leaves, the Roman wall and the distant tunnels and earth forts 'with the usual touch of melancholy that a past-marked prospect lends' (p. 126). Things are kept in perspective. The landscape contains both the living and reminders of the dead.

To give his language a wider range of suggestion Hardy uses references from many sources. They include classical authors, British authors ranging from Shakespeare to Hardy's contemporary, Tennyson, painters and their individual works, popular songs and, most significantly for this novel, the Bible. There are several references to Old Testament prophets and great men, including Samson. The parallels between Henchard and Farfrae and Saul and David have been mentioned elsewhere, with Henchard acting as irrationally as Saul. Henchard also associates himself with the archetypal figure Cain. Cain's punishment was more than he could bear but Henchard rises defiantly above his situation (p. 269). At appropriate moments, such as significant chapter endings, Hardy's prose even takes on the sonorous rhythm of Biblical prose, as for example, in Mother Cuxsom's elegy on the death of Susan, and especially Henchard's final turning his back upon Casterbridge.

Then, before she could collect her thoughts, Henchard went out from her rooms, and departed from the house by the back way as he had come; and she saw him no more.

5.3 CHARACTERISATION

Michael Henchard

Henchard begins the novel by entering as if on to the stage, 'with the walk of a skilled countryman', at his side his dependants, evidence of marriage and status in society. He ends the novel by 'wambling' away from Casterbridge, alone and anxious only for death. He introduces himself by an irresponsible, cruel act, breaking the major convention that holds society together, then falls asleep, snoring drunkenly across a table. It is not an auspicious introduction. Yet when he finally leaves Casterbridge it is as a tragic figure with whom we are completely involved and for whom we feel an infinite pity. The account of his death is magnificently told and moving in the extreme. He has been compared to the great tragic heroes of classical drama and, given an expanded concept of the three unities of time, place and action acceptable in a novel, there are parallels in the manner in which he dominates the story and pursues a seemingly inevitable fate. If the first chapters are accepted as Prologue then the main drama is concentrated into a brief, intense period of decline and fall, compared to the many years off-stage of his rise. He has also been compared with Shakespeare's King Lear, alone on the heath with his Fool, another great tragic figure who brought his fate down upon himself by an initial rash and unkind act. This places Henchard very high in the ranks of tragic heroes, in spite of his humble origins. What is it about this apparently primitive man that compels our interest and in the end our sadness?

He is isolated from the beginning, towering above his family – Susan came up to his shoulder – ignoring them and pretending to read a ballad sheet. Ballads dealt with the dramatic and unusual rather than the mundane. Marriage has been two years of stale familiarity punctuated by temper and threats. His is phlegmatic, supercilious and, inside the furmity tent, he shows 'the instinct of a perverse character'. Drinking heavily, he becomes 'brilliantly', and overbearingly, quarrelsome. Self-indulgently, he bemoans his marriage, broadcasts his ambition and, on a drunken impulse which will not let him draw back, auctions his wife and child. He has threatened before but this time has tempted fate once too often. Quite literally out of the blue, a buyer appears, pays hard cash and disappears with his purchase. Fate and temperament have combined to set Henchard free to pursue his ambition. At this stage the novelty of the situation ensures our continued interest in the man.

He wakes up to a new dawn and a new life, and immediately shows another side to his character. Anger argues with remorse, but he is above all determined to put things right. He will always accept responsibility for what he has done. Something akin to pagan compulsion makes him swear a greater oath than ever before, indicating that oath-swearing and superstition influence him. His search, on as large a scale as he could manage, becomes a crusade. We note the reluctant spending of the sailor's money. We have a complex character, only twenty-one admittedly, but age does not seem significant. He is given to gestures very much larger than life, a mixture of wild impulsiveness and dogged determination. He has been isolated as a pilgrim who takes us with him 'in a new direction' (p. 39).

We see him next at the height of his municipal career as Mayor. His 'amazing energy' (p. 113) had ensured success. Yet, at the head of a prosperous borough he stands apart. At a function, presumably one of many, where everyone drinks copiously, he stands alone. His empty glasses indicate great strength of will, and formidable resolution. We learn that collectively he had benefited the Corporation but that as individuals he had made many of them 'wince' (p. 113). He is dressed and decorated for the part but socially he is someone whose laughter no one shares. The respect he commanded is beginning to wane; he dominates the proceedings but there is tension in his exchanges with his fellow-citizens. There is little

genuine warmth surrounding the Mayor. We look in and view him dispassionately.

The stranger, Farfrae, symbolises a friendship that Henchard has never
had and he must own him by bidding and then raising his bid, as if Farfrae
were a piece of property. The possessiveness indicates a basic insecurity.
Everything is done on a grand scale, even to Farfrae's being almost forcibly
over-fed. Henchard, desperate to talk to someone, takes the much younger
man into his confidence. He asks Farfrae little about himself. We begin to
understand his loneliness. Susan and Elizabeth-Jane offer him a new family
circle. He makes up for the past as far as his money can make amends but,
sadly, he is unable to establish a personal relationship; he cannot, for
example, convey his genuine admiration to Elizabeth-Jane, ' 'Od send –
I've nothing to say to 'i' (p. 94).

He is his own worst enemy. 'Character is Fate' Hardy quotes but leaves
open the question how far character and how far fate combine to deprive
him gradually, not only of everything he had laboriously built up over the
years, but also the promise of family happiness, including a relationship
that could have resembled father and son. The Whittle affair shows
Henchard at his worst, except that he did look after Whittle's mother. But
had he thus bought Whittle? The break with Farfrae is the result of overwhelming jealousy promoting words regretted as soon as uttered. Henchard,
however, never goes back on anything. He becomes increasingly unsure
and plunges into imprudent business deals based on superstitious nonsense.
The weather-prophet exploits a child-like strain in his character. Chance
decrees that he open Susan's letter, that Lucetta should come to High-
Place Hall and that the furmity woman should find her way to Casterbridge
court. To his increasingly desperate attempts to preserve his position are
added these dramatic blows. Are they more than Henchard deserved? He
is down but not out. We forget the petty involvement with Jopp and
admire the dignity of the retreat from the court and the scrupulous
honesty and generosity of the bankruptcy scene.

He is, however, unstable; no mood lasts for long. We are involved with
him and sympathetic but annoyed, angered and repulsed as well. He is now
alone, the tenant of despised Jopp, in an isolated cottage. He has failed
with every human being of any consequence in his life. What follows is his
climb back from the depths, a process which shows him advancing and
falling back as a human being, learning to love someone outside himself
and in doing so earning our respect and sympathy. Everything is still done
on an epic scale or taken to the extreme. When he drinks it leads to his
domination of the choir and the 'curse' psalm in 'The Three Mariners'.
His physical presence is still intimidating.

A whim makes him ask to join the procession for the Royal Personage;
refusal turns the whim into determination. The irresponsible Henchard

subsequently becomes a potential murderer but disarms credulity by his tying one arm behind his back. He might murder Farfrae, and in his view it would be a fair fight, but does the reader imagine that it will end in deliberate death? We are beginning to know Henchard and remember that he could not betray Lucetta in cold blood. In some ways he is a great child, with a child's wayward demands and reactions, and as a child he resents being supplanted in areas where he had reigned supreme. Yet there is the element of absolute honesty, the marvellous dignity and even delicacy of manner that he can assume, and the inability to take ultimate advantage of anyone, especially someone he had loved.

The fight marks a watershed in the presentation of Henchard. Hitherto he has dominated the novel largely by a mixture of aggression and possessive kindness. Yet, even after the fight, as he runs alongside Farfrae's gig, gasping out his unheeded warning, we feel that he is essentially a good man. Farfrae's understandable spurning of the message adds an irony that increases our sympathy. This is Henchard's first completely unselfish act, carried out with all his usual impulse and determination, and it is rejected.

Chapter Forty-one begins with Henchard going home, lighting his fire and sitting by it 'abstractedly'. He is beginning to examine himself. Elizabeth-Jane calls, his one contact in the world, and sleeps while her supposed father lies to Newson. The lie is completely out of character, or out of his 'old' character, the reaction of a man who is now desperately lonely, as he tells Elizabeth-Jane, 'to a degree that you know nothing of'. He then adds 'It is my own fault', a sentence of self-realisation which accepts the consequences. He has been thinking to some effect. Elizabeth-Jane represents affection that he now realises to be the most precious quality he has ever been offered. Consistent in his reactions to the last, he will prize it with an extreme enthusiasm.

Brought back from the brink of suicide, and for the moment convinced that he is not forgotten by a loving God, he achieves a precarious happiness with Elizabeth-Jane. He is humble in demeanour, the old, 'leonine' look giving way to that of the 'netted lion' (p. 261). His attitudes change; he devotes all thought and energy to harmony. Cruelly, his perceptions are sharpened. He suffers anguish from Elizabeth-Jane's growing relationship with Farfrae. His anguish is heightened by the acceptance that he has no right to interfere (p. 263). We remember his letters to Farfrae peremptorily rejecting, then inviting, overtures to Elizabeth-Jane and realise how far he has travelled in self-awareness and self-abnegation.

The return of Newson, however, means final isolation for Henchard. He must move on because there seems no place for him in Casterbridge. His pride is now that of the stoic. He has brought about the situation and he will accept the consequences. Elizabeth-Jane's reproach would kill him metaphorically so he must break with the only contact that had promised harmony. He goes with simple words which suggest his new understanding of the past and the present, 'though I loved 'ee late, I loved 'ee well' (p. 268).

Henchard, now absolutely alone in an anonymous landscape, broods continually, not on an ambitious return to prosperity but only on a renewal of his association with Elizabeth-Jane. His penultimate, great impulse takes him to the wedding. The depiction of the man, desperate for loving-kindness, gazing through a half-opened door at the wedding-dance so full of life is Hardy's most poignant use of the looking-in technique. Farfrae dances freely, Newson is completely lost in carefree abandonment. The man capable of the deepest feelings has no place in the circle. Pathetically anxious to find even a small place for himself he yet cannot bring himself to plead. His final impulse takes him away, any defence abandoned, a last speech being a movingly dignified blend of pride and humility before the tragic journey. And we know that he will keep his word.

There was no place for Henchard in the domestic Casterbridge of Elizabeth-Jane and Farfrae. Yet we are left with a sense of waste, of something rare and awe-inspiring being lost to the everyday world.

In that world Elizabeth-Jane will personify balance and the ultimate reward of virtue. Donald Farfrae will be one in a line of Mayors, remembered for progressive views and possibly the establishment of a limited company. Henchard will belong to another world of legend, a life and death which moves us to anger and to sadness but never to indifference.

Elizabeth-Jane

Elizabeth-Jane is the principal female character yet her status and situation are made the least secure. She lives in six different houses in the novel. At one stage she can hesitantly but happily learn the art of fashionable dressing but later she has stoically to pack away the fine dresses of her palmy days and resume the humble task of netting (p. 202). But she is also the character whom Hardy chooses to end the novel, when he gives details of her future life and philosophy in what is essentially an epilogue to the death of Henchard, and which ensures that a balanced, if less dramatic, way of life is carried on.

The key word is balance – learned from sometimes bitter experience, supplemented, perhaps, by such wisdom as can be gained by reading. She is the one person to whom books are important. Hardy makes her experience many roles: as a commentator on the market scene; as an onlooker from her small lodgings; as a companion to Lucetta; as a judge of men when she warns Henchard not to employ Jopp, as a worried daughter warning Farfrae about Henchard, her sense of duty overcoming her reluctance; as the upholder of a rigid sense of morality and, always, as the one person who consistently stands by Henchard when he is really down. She seems to make a fetish of respectability but is not too proud to wait at table. Of all the characters, she successfully bridges the gap between employer and servant.

She is rarely off the scene in the novel, becoming increasingly prominent in the second half. As mentioned above, she is someone who watches, apparently outside the match-making but reporting on it, or putting it into perspective. Or, she will be there to help at a moment of crisis, as when Lucetta catches sight of the skimmington-ride. Something of a Cinderella, a good fairy, with a suggestion of Florence Nightingale, she is also like St Luke, 'the evangelist who had to write it all down' (p. 166).

Given all these virtues, Elizabeth-Jane could well appear to be too good to be true. Hardy makes her the proponent of an austere morality, using exceptionally strong language. 'Her craving for correctness of procedure was, indeed, almost vicious' (p. 193). True, he qualifies this by putting forward her mother's marital history as the cause (though we are never clear how much Elizabeth-Jane knew) but it is an instance of unswerving opinion, confirmed by the later confrontation with Lucetta. The counterbalance to this however is her complete lack of pretension. This is not lack of spirit because she does leave Henchard initially, to his surprise, and also leaves Lucetta in a very decided manner, finding lodgings for herself and maintaining herself with great independence of spirit.

The lack of pretension, also the air of calm associated with her, spring from a habit of reflection. She is the one character who does reflect dispassionately on what she sees. A seer's spirit can take possession of her (p. 159). As a result general reflections on life itself are associated with her. 'Life is tragical rather than comical' is a sad conclusion to arrive at after hearing Farfrae sing; the moments of gladness are never the equal of those of pain. In another mood she can sit at her mother's bedside and send herself to sleep with abstruse philosophical questions to which there is no answer (p. 117). Are these and other deliberations on the quality and purpose of life the thoughts of Hardy himself? Elizabeth-Jane's conclusions involve a wryly-humorous acceptance of what life offers; she has her share of disappointed hopes, particularly with her early feelings for Farfrae, but achieves a certain equanimity by never giving up hope.

Ironically it is the lesser townsfolk who recognise and comment on her quality (p. 233). She suffers because she is linked with Henchard. Yet here she is playing her most important role in the novel because it is through her that Henchard begins himself to learn self-awareness. Because of her Henchard begins to think of someone other than himself; because of her he learns to love another human being. Her logic is very simple. When Henchard has been on the point of committing suicide, at his lowest ebb, he returns to find Elizabeth-Jane waiting for him – she knew that everything seemed against him and that he must be suffering. It is worth quoting the effect she had, expressed by Hardy once more with Biblical rhythm:

> Then Henchard shaved for the first time during many days, and put on clean linen, and combed his hair; and was as a man resuscitated thenceforward. (p. 258)

Of course, being Henchard, no emotion he feels can be anything but on a grand scale and his love for Elizabeth-Jane becomes an obsession, his very reason for living. Yet on account of her he must leave Casterbridge. She is the motivating force of the tragedy, his most treasured possession whom he knows he must renounce. She watches him leave Casterbridge with unfeigned wonder and sorrow; Hardy adds the poignant little detail that she kept him back a minute or two before finally letting him go (p. 269).

Elizabeth-Jane has been criticised for her rejection of Henchard at the wedding reception. It is true that her speech is a bitter outpouring of accusation with wounding phrases like 'my warm-hearted real father' seemingly emphasising the rejection. It could be argued that this is in keeping with her strict appreciation of right and wrong, emphasised earlier in the novel. Yet she drew her hand from his 'gently' before speaking and the last sentence indicates that she has not forgotten the great love that there was between them.

Henchard will neither justify nor plead but answers with his last impulsive words. Elizabeth-Jane is not given time to collect her thoughts before he goes. Would the outcome have been different if she had been given time?

The end of the novel is something of an anticlimax in that the greatness has gone and we are left with the world continuing at a lower intensity. It is Elizabeth-Jane's world. She has achieved stability and increasing wisdom. She has emerged from the tragedy with as optimistic a message as Hardy ever gives us, that the 'general drama of pain' may be the occasional episode and not the whole. Morally, Elizabeth-Jane deserves her happiness. Symbolically she represents a balanced and secure married life emerging from the marital complications gone before. Typically, however, she takes nothing for granted, experience has taught her the unpredictability of life.

Donald Farfrae

Ruddy and of fair countenance, bright-eyed and slight of build (p. 54), Farfrae's entry into the novel coincides exactly with the discussion on poor corn and bread in 'The King's Arms', and he is drawn into the story by an impulsive act of generosity. He is an immediate social success, his spontaneous charm enabling him to penetrate an established centre of Casterbridge social life and captivate a not uncritical audience with his singing. He seems to have a magic that is new to Casterbridge, with echoes of a mysterious land far to the north. Though young, he has seen more than the average Casterbridge citizen, passing through the boundaries of the town (which Hardy is careful to circumscribe most accurately) on the way to more exotic shores. Wandering minstrel, pilgrim to lands overseas, mysterious stranger, Farfrae is the ambitious, adventurous embodiment of the migrant urge. Hardy's comparison of him to a poet of a new school (p. 67) is apt; it is as if Farfrae brings forgotten romance back into Casterbridge life, with a loosening of inhibition and spreading of spontaneity. Singing, and later dancing, are largely his province in the novel.

The romantic element, however, is balanced by the classical restraint of making money. From the beginning the mixture of occasional 'odd gravity' and romantic sentiment is emphasised. His songs entrance the evening drinkers but commercially he brings new business practices which are far more significant. He is a new man in that he is obviously educated, good at science and its practical applications, and aware of technological development in agriculture. He is meticulous in his business practice, with ledgers and receipt books, accurate measurement and calculated buying policies, not all of which were common in Casterbridge. He becomes involved in the traditional activities of the area with a new approach and a new success. His influence will spread so that early in his Casterbridge career he will head a group organising public entertainment; Casterbridge residents will follow him willingly. In a remarkably short space of time he will be listed as eventual Mayor: when the position becomes vacant following an emergency, shortly afterwards he, almost automatically, is the nominee. He has made good.

Yet he is, of course, the lesser Mayor of the novel and we follow his meteoric rise with Henchard in mind. The paths of the two men have similarities. Both move to Casterbridge, both are ambitious, both achieve great success, though Farfrae's is far more rapid. He arrives in Casterbridge just as Henchard's dominance is threatened, the old king of ancient myth to be replaced by the new; Saul to be usurped by David. David is described as 'ruddy and of a fair countenance' when he comes to the court of Saul (1 Samuel 17.42). Farfrae seems to have all the qualities that Henchard lacks. He is calm and rational in his approach; he has an even temper, is polite and considerate. He is scrupulously fair in his dealings with other businessmen and attentive to the welfare of his workmen. He is meticulous over detail yet can cast an imaginative eye at the future. He makes a good Mayor, controlling meetings with tact and handling the crisis with Henchard firmly when the royal visit is threatened. He does not bear malice and repeatedly tries to befriend Henchard. He can act most generously, as when he hires the old shepherd as well as his son to prevent their being split up. And at the end of the novel he will accede to Elizabeth-Jane's request and drive her in search of Henchard.

With such a paragon of virtue why are we not more involved in his success? Is it because he becomes less spontaneous as we get to know him better? Is there an element of calculation in everything he does? He would never marry before he could afford to do so, unlike Henchard, who married early and spent two years regretting it. He can disturb Elizabeth-Jane's equanimity by half-proposing to her after the dance but withdraw prudently a moment later. Eventually he can decide when the money is made, that she will do because she is 'pleasing, thrifty and satisfactory' (p. 148), a curious trio of recommendations.

He is at his most vulnerable when he meets Lucetta. She had not met any man like him before and he certainly had not met any woman like her. The two sides of his character are emphasised by Hardy as Farfrae hovers between mercantile and romantic moods. He is completely happy singing inside the seed-drill; Lucetta's comment sums up the complexities of his character:

'The "Lass of Gowrie" from inside of a seed-drill – what a phenomenon!' (p. 157).

The 'phenomenon' is successful in everything he undertakes and ultimately has gained everything that Henchard has lost. It is possible, however, to make too much of his calculating manner. He is a good master, even though he reduces wages. His workmen preferred stability and consistent attitudes to storm and a little more money. He was ready to leave Henchard over the Whittle affair. He made Lucetta a considerate husband, though business meant being away a great deal. And if Coney and Longways did not think so highly of him as Mayor as when a man sitting in 'The Three Mariners', that is normal human reaction and they were anxious to spare him pain.

The mercantile side of his nature is more stressed in the second half of the book. Success means less romance. The death of Lucetta brings desire for revenge but a carefully-argued paragraph ends with Farfrae's reconciling consideration and philosophy, and determining to do nothing. He considers the profit and loss account of the marriage, looks forward to what future balance sheets might have been and is not long in pursuing the more solid promise of Elizabeth-Jane once again. And all does proceed satisfactorily to a business-like conclusion. We have a last glimpse of the romantic Farfrae dancing at the wedding and a final commonsense but somehow inappropriate comment on the change from a sovereign. His reaction to Henchard's death is one of muted incomprehension.

Farfrae is sometimes written down in order that Henchard might be written up but Farfrae's very normality, his good points and what he makes of them, must be stressed so that Henchard is seen to exit imaginatively on another plane. Farfrae joins the long line of Mayors who kept

Casterbridge prosperous, pushing the town into the machine age. Henchard, for better or worse, was so much more.

Lucetta

Henchard calls her 'an artful little woman' (p.141) approving 'Lucetta's adroit and pleasant manoeuvre' with Elizabeth-Jane. This reflects no credit on Henchard or Lucetta and our initial impressions of her are coloured by this willingness to use the trust of others to her own selfish advantage. She emerges from Henchard's past, on her own admission flighty and unsettled, with a gay but unstable back-ground, despised because she is poor. She and Henchard were lonely. Presumably Henchard offered some promise of stability. She matched him impulse for impulse; indiscretion and scandal followed in the time-honoured manner of Victorian melo-drama. He had to leave, vowing allegiance; she wrote compromising letters, emphasising her own misery.

Fate ironically decides that Lucetta shall have money, which gives her the power to establish herself and buy stability. She is drawn back to Henchard and Casterbridge. Her letters (Hardy writes that she was rather addicted to scribbling) become a vital part of the plot, carried about, left, and finally exposed to ridicule. In Casterbridge she appears sophisticated, symbolically taking High-Place Hall, ordering fashionable furniture, buying many clothes and suffering pseudo-agonies over what to wear. Her taste inclines to the bright, if not the garish. It is all rather calculated, as are her poses taken up to receive callers, 'flinging herself on the couch in the cyma-recta curve which so became her' (p. 147). Henchard is accepted because he is the best there is.

The plot requires love at first sight and the impulsive Lucetta falls for Farfrae. Henchard can be easily abandoned. She will marry beneath her but is happy to find someone she can love and someone who seems capable of organising her life in an harmonious pattern. She does need someone to cling to.

Initially that person is Elizabeth-Jane. She receives Lucetta's first confidences and is with her when she falls in the fit. A comparative study of the two women would help establish the characters of both. Lucetta is calculating, coquettish, and self-absorbed, yet beneath the exterior she is unsure, even timid, and liable to completely irrational behaviour.

She achieves her aim but, ironically, does not enjoy long the social prestige of being the Mayor's wife. She does not seem to belong to the community, being seen usually in her house, waiting for Farfrae. Her death is reported, her funeral details are not even mentioned. This is in sharp contrast to the death of Susan Henchard. Lucetta dies unavenged – for everybody's sake. She could have been a nuisance even after death but she is quickly forgotten.

Susan Henchard

Susan seems the least sharply defined of the three major women characters, lacking the potential of Elizabeth-Jane or the sparkle of Lucetta. Yet she can be driven to forthright action as when she flings the wedding ring at Henchard, the culmination of two years of his temper and recrimination. Her appearance must have attracted him, an attraction of opposites, but her very meekness and bird-like chirpings (p. 31), would antagonise Henchard. Her appreciation of life was that it was uncertain and unfair. She passed on to her daughter her looks, a certain sense of propriety and an independence of spirit which had been all but quelled in her by Henchard.

She recognised her daughter's aspirations and it is repeatedly emphasised that she went to Casterbridge mainly for the sake of Elizabeth-Jane; for herself she wanted nothing. It has been argued that she is shrewd, unscrupulous, even cunning, because of her keeping the secret of Elizabeth Jane's parentage from Henchard (and, incidentally, from the reader so that it makes for a fine dramatic revelation). However, this, and the letter to Farfrae, indicate the overwhelming determination to help Elizabeth-Jane and make her independent of Henchard. She anticipated only too well his reaction to Elizabeth-Jane as Newson's daughter. Her moving letter to Henchard indicates a greater depth of character than we have seen developed.

She is an integral part of the novel's beginning. She vanishes, returns, and represents reconciliation, but at the same time leaves behind that which destroys the harmony created. Her death and the badly-sealed letter dramatically change the relationships of Henchard and Elizabeth-Jane. The funeral chorus give us details of her concern that everything should be correct. Her last words were of Elizabeth-Jane and her epitaph is an elegiac speech in fine Biblical cadences from Mother Cuxsom, whom we normally associate with blame rather than sympathy.

Richard Newson

Another of the novel's wanderers, Newson, a generous man with his money, casually looks into the furmity tent and almost as casually it seems, on an impulse 'buys' Susan and the baby. He thought they might be happier with him. His temperament being the exact opposite of Henchard's, he does bring her happiness and when her doubts begin he respects her scruples and conveniently disappears. If he were a more developed character we would want to go deeper into his motives. As it is, through a chance encounter he begins the buying and selling in the book and his ready money, of which he always seems to have plenty, turns the auction 'joke' into reality.

Appearing as the mysterious stranger at 'Peter's Finger,' Newson adds an air of expectation to the plot, though the skimmington-ride and its consequences banish him for the moment. Always good-humoured, lively and outgoing, he was prepared to help the skimmington-ride because it promised amusement. He is the complete extrovert compared to Henchard the introvert. He is friendly and trusting in Henchard's presence, accepting his word about Elizabeth-Jane's death, then disappearing again. This time he does go out with heavy tread. This time, too, we can suppose that he will be back. His presence disturbed Henchard; his absence drives him to distraction.

His final jovial acceptance of Henchard's deception seems odd, even for someone as amiable as Newson – in sharp contrast to Elizabeth-Jane's shocked response. He seems most interested in the convivial aspects of the wedding, with an eagerness that makes Farfrae seem puritanical. His final appearance in the tableau of the wedding dance emphasises how much a part of it he is and how much he enjoys it. To those inside it is a dance full of life and promise, to Henchard outside, supplanted at the end as in the beginning by Newson, it suggests only isolation and emptiness.

Having served his purpose and demonstrated his inability to remain still, Newson is arbitrarily settled at Budmouth. Ironically, having found his daughter, he is never in close contact with her. The 'father' figure must remain Henchard.

The urban chorus

In earlier Wessex novels, Hardy often used a group of minor characters, agricultural workers and villagers, as a form of chorus, adding information and commentary on the action in the manner of the chorus in ancient Greek drama, though Hardy's use was comic rather than tragic. His rustics also added strong local colour, provided down-to-earth humour and ironic comment on those more important than themselves. Casterbridge will have an urban chorus but its functions are the same. Solomon Longways, Christopher Coney, Buzzford, Mother Cuxsom and Nance Mockridge appear frequently amid the crowd, to fill in the background or put a collective point of view. Nance Mockridge exhibits the 'unprincipled bread', Coney and Longways give Henchard's history and hint that he is making a mistake. All are present at Henchard's wedding and Susan's funeral, with traditional comment and stories that are becoming legends, the burial of the unpretentious woman loosening the threads of reminiscence and sympathetic philosophy. They represent the working classes of Casterbridge, men employed by Henchard and Farfrae, women concerned with the quality of their bread.

Yet Hardy's Casterbridge chorus is not as simple as that. There is Mixen Lane, a reminder that below the prosperous community life there is a life of poverty and squalor. Jopp and the furmity woman gravitate there; Charl would cheerfully rob Newson of his sovereigns there. Nance Mockridge and Mother Cuxsom reign in 'Peter's Finger', and are instrumental in planning the skimmington-ride. The unemployed, the discomfited and the grudge-bearers decline to Mixen Lane, by no means a friendly chorus. Distinctions are made; Coney and Longways save Farfrae from the impact of the ride, Mother Cuxsom is jolly rather than vindictive, unlike Nance who is a virago, but the overall attitude of the chorus is critical, submerged in the sombre tone of the novel.

6 SPECIMEN PASSAGE AND COMMENTARY

By close inspection of a selected passage it is possible to appreciate just how rich and evocative Hardy can be in his writing, both from the immediate impact of the passage itself and from its general reference outwards to the rest of the novel. The following closely-linked paragraphs offer a good example of fine descriptive writing together with many suggestive allusions to main themes in the novel. They are taken from Chapter 36.

The lane and its surrounding thicket of thatched cottages stretched out like a spit into the moist and misty lowland. Much that was sad, much that was low, some things that were baneful, could be seen in Mixen Lane. Vice ran freely in and out of certain doors of the neighbourhood: recklessness dwelt under the roof with the crooked chimney: shame in some bow-windows: theft (in times of privation) in the thatched and mud-walled houses by the gallows. Even slaughter had not been altogether unknown here. In a block of cottages up an alley there might have been erected an altar to disease in years gone by. Such was Mixen Lane in the times when Henchard and Farfrae were Mayors.

Yet this mildewed leaf in the sturdy and flourishing Casterbridge plant lay close to the open country; not a hundred yards from a row of noble elms and commanding a view across the moor of airy uplands and corn-fields, and mansions of the great. A brook divided the moor from the tenements and to outward view there was no way across it – no way to the houses but round about by the road. But under every householder's stairs there was kept a mysterious plank nine inches wide; which plank was a secret bridge.

If you, as one of those refugee householders, came in from business after dark – and this was the business time here – you stealthily crossed the moor, approached the border of the aforesaid brook, and whistled opposite the house to which you belonged. A shape thereupon made its appearance on the other side bearing the bridge on end against the sky;

it was lowered; you crossed, and a hand helped you to land yourself, together with the pheasants and hares gathered from neighbouring manors. You sold them slily the next morning, and the day after you stood before the magistrates with the eyes of all your sympathising neighbours concentrated on your back. You disappeared for a time; then you were again found quietly living in Mixen Lane.

For some critics the town of Casterbridge is as important as the Mayor himself. Hardy goes to immense pains to create a real and living community with its business and its buildings – offices, churches, halls, homes and public houses, together with the flowers and trees which surround them and give them shade and colour, as often as not in bright morning or gentle evening light. These points have relevance because in sharp contrast these paragraphs are almost completely devoid of colour and beauty; the little colour suggested is out of reach of the people concerned and the general impression is darkness not light.

The paragraphs describe Mixen Lane, the antithesis of Casterbridge's Corn Street. The first sentence suggests something vague and unhealthy. The alliteration on 'thatched' and 'thicket' underlines the muffled, secretive quality of this settlement; 'spit' is sharp and distinctive but only in contrast with the damp. indistinct landscape, low in every respect. Whatsoever things are sad, low and baneful, rather than things of virtue and of good report, are found here. The Biblical echo (Philippians, Chapter 4, Verse 7) is found in the pattern and rhythm of Hardy's sentence. Personification is used to emphasise the general characteristics of the community; vice, rather than virtue, is the standard of neighbourliness. A misshapen chimney rises above wayward lives; bay-windows, a symbol of pride elsewhere, reveal the opposite here. Often, theft is the only answer to poverty to support walls made from and rising from the damp lands, shaded by trees whose very name can only help reinforce the unwholesome atmosphere in which the inhabitants live. Life is cheap and wholesale destroyers of life such as cholera make homage to death rather than life seem more appropriate.

Mixen Lane is Casterbridge's human septic tank. It is immediately adjacent to the bare expanse of Durnover Moor, uninviting and unproductive, but is separated even from that by a brook which acts as a moat, defining and protecting the lane. Hardy uses natural imagery. Casterbridge is compared to a sturdy, flourishing plant but Mixen Lane hangs on to the healthy plant like a mildewed leaf and of course mildew is a spreading infection if not checked. The creeping implications are obvious. The lane looks across to the moor, the interim wasteland, to a growth of fine trees, dignified by the adjective 'noble', ordered and upright, symbols of another world. The uplands are airy and therefore healthy, with no place for mildew. The cornfields are presumably also thriving, examples of organised industry and rich landscape. From the lane they can be seen but only to be envied. The mansions and the great people who live in them, great because of their wealth springing from the ownership of the land, exemplify the rigid social divisions of this world. The lowest can glimpse the establishments of the great, so near in distance, so impossible of attainment.

Rhythm and vocabulary contribute powerfully to the effect of Hardy's sentences. The muted sound of 'mildewed leaf' is balanced by the 'sturdy and flourishing', reinforcing the sharp contrast in growth. The flow of the first long sentence of the second paragraph sweeps across an attractive, open landscape, with pleasant variety and open to the sky. The tone changes with the dividing brook; 'no way to the houses but round by the road' underlines by its length and rhythm the tortuous way in. Once there the tone changes again to the subdued note appropriate to something secret under the stairs.

The singular secret, latent during the day, is the centrepiece of a nightly ritual peculiar to Mixen Lane. The planks, precisely measured to be just wide enough for the purpose, and of the same pattern throughout the lane, have felt countless experienced crossings in a grand conspiracy of silence. Hardy makes the reader part of the conspiracy, 'you' are there; yet you still remain an observer, able to watch with fascination the performing of the ritual, then drawn across the bridge into the carefully-guarded recess.

It is all a matter of property and business. Casterbridge is all business; we remember the many bustling market scenes in the morning, afternoon and early evening, but after dark business ceases and the lamps light up the streets. That business is largely in corn, buying and selling with rubbing shoulders in the Corn Exchange and the signing of cheques. The corn comes from the fields that can be seen from Mixen Lane but its inhabitants have no business there. There is no market day and no legal currency. Nothing is above board save the nocturnal tread across the plank, silent and obscure.

For it is all shadowy. There are no 'loud' words in the beginning of the second paragraph except the 'whistle', which would be low and swift. The movement is steady but careful, everything goes according to plan. A vague shape rising out of the moor, you contact an equally vague outline across the brook, only the plank briefly stark against the sky. An anonymous hand (names would identify people) helps you 'land', a word suggestive of a voyager back from a foraging trip, having sailed back from the rich plantations beyond the moor. It is low-key business with appropriate vocabulary. Refugee business, carried on 'stealthily', after dark. It remains anonymous, 'you' do this, 'you' do that, nothing precise except the plank with its suggestion of piracy. The outer world intrudes with the hares and pheasant, recognisably colourful creatures, but they disappear into the shadows. Symbolically, they had presumably belonged to a gentleman of the light, his possessions along with his mansion; now they belong to the creatures of the dark, crossing the drawbridge into the keep of Mixen Lane.

Morning transforms the shadows into men bent on regular business. They sell their booty in public. 'Slily' suggests taking a chance but being ever watchful, also a market for such poached produce with perhaps nobody too anxious to hear the origin of the game. We imagine an established routine of disposal, with its own code, and then back to 'Peter's Finger' with the proceeds. Yet the almost romantic picture dissolves with Hardy's cryptic summarising of the results of the night's work, an excellent illustration of much suggested in little.

The shady figure of the night is arrested and brought into the full light of the court. He is obviously well-known and has been careless or unlucky. The pattern is familiar to the constables and magistrates. In a few words we have the criminal before the Bench of Magistrates (which included Henchard and Grower) with all Mixen Lane exuding sympathy behind him. The court was a place of public entertainment and many from the lane would have been star performers themselves. Prison does not deter however and the prisoner returns to Mixen Lane, keeping a low profile by day but caught up in the old ritual again by night.

There is a more sinister aspect suggested by the paragraphs. It is very much a world of the rich and the poor, the world of the mansion and the hovel, with a society organised to protect the hares and the pheasants from those who have little or nothing. Mixen Lane is a ghetto, and ghettoes breed envy and discontent. It is such a sharp contrast to the rest of Casterbridge that it can only be a potential threat. From an individual poaching expedition we are taken to the majesty of the law and the penal system. The threat becomes real in the skimmington-ride, an aggressive challenge to the law and the social order it supports.

7 CRITICAL APPRAISALS

7.1 CRITICAL APPRAISALS

The Mayor of Casterbridge was written during 1884 and finished on 17 April, 1885. It was serialised weekly in The *Graphic* from January to May 1886 and first published in book form on 10 May 1886. By this time, of course, Hardy was an established author and could expect reviews in the leading periodicals and literary magazines of the day. It was not a book on which there was any general agreement, reviewers dividing into distinct camps, with a general reaction of slight disappointment. The general public were tardy in buying; about 600 copies from the first edition were sold, 158 were remaindered. Six years after publication an American academic reviewer found it 'the least attractive of all Hardy's books' which, he adds, the booksellers found to be unpopular.

Some comments from contemporary periodicals will indicate how the reviewers interpreted Hardy to their readers. It would be worthwhile to consider how relevant the points are to our own appreciation or criticism of the novel today. Does Hardy seem to speak to us with the same voice? Do we raise the same critical issues in our discussion of the novel?

The *Saturday Review* (29 May 1886) found the book disappointing. It complained of the story. This was stated to be very slight and singularly devoid of context while at the same time being too improbable. The reviewer thought, however, that Casterbridge could not have been done better and that the peasants (sic) were admirable, with their dialogue the only feature lifting the weight of the novel. He especially praised the funeral conversation of Mother Cuxsom and Solomon Longways. He could, however, find no individual character capable of raising even a passing interest. Plot, characters, background, peasant chorus and dialect form the substance of the reviews. Would you dismiss Hardy's handling of most of these as ineffectual?

The *Athenaeum* (29 May 1886) reviewer was more discerning. He praised Hardy's ingenuity in convincing the reader that 'an improbable situation may be probable'. Hardy, too, was confirmed as a superb story-teller, creating characters that were so real that they often were thought of as having a life beyond the book. Class implications are found in the following quotation:

> He has a wonderful knowledge of the minds of men and women, particularly those belonging to a class which better-educated people are often disposed to imagine has no mind.

This, at least, is a progressive viewpoint going beyond the notion that all country-dwellers are yokels. The writer, is, however, critical of Henchard as hero. The book will not be popular because it is 'the tragedy (if it may be so called) of a self-willed instead of unselfish hero'. The writer has a dogmatic approach to heroism, obviously. Is there any justification for this point of view? Is Henchard selfish?

He then raised the question of the language of the peasants in the novel. He found it 'neither dialect exactly produced nor a thorough tendering into educated English', also accusing Hardy of being inconsistent in his characters' use of dialect, which diminishes the reader's satisfaction. Was the critic being too critical? How far should an author compromise in this area? The writer also complained about 'far-fetched and unpleasant similes and epithets citing as examples 'the sun was resting on the hill like a drop of blood on an eyelid' (p. 220) and 'the espaliers . . . had pulled their stakes out of the ground, and stood distorted and writhing in vegetable agony, like leafy Laocoons' (p. 84). Effective or overdone? Is exaggeration a common tendency in Hardy?

A very long review in the influential *Spectator* (5 June 1886) objects to Henchard as 'a man of character' suggesting rather that Henchard has no fixed character at all. He then goes on to write with generous enthusiasm on Henchard, as powerful a study as any Hardy has created, 'a man of large nature and depth of passion, who is yet subject to the most fitful influences'. He elaborates at length on his complexities and inconsistencies. He argues that with a little more firm character Henchard's nature would have been one of 'gigantic mould' with enormous potential, but that Hardy's purpose was to show a nature running mostly to waste. Henchard's 'tragic mobility of mood' leads to extremes of temperament. The strong impression is of reality as well as homely grandeur, almost magnificent.

The one complaint is of Hardy's 'fashionable pessimism'. Hardy should not introduce throughout the novel hints of philosophical speculations that were out of place in this context. He quotes, 'the ingenious machinery contrived by the gods for reducing human possibilities of amelioration to a minimum' (p. 274) as pagan and misleading. He is arguing, of course, from a Christian viewpoint. Yet Henchard had captured his imagination.

He admires Elizabeth-Jane though thinks that the subdued tone of the character makes her seem a little tame. Farfrae is vivid but too cold-blooded, so very inferior to the master whom he supplants. 'Why do we like the Scotsman so little?' The answer probably lies in his unreserved praise of Henchard and 'the portrayal of the apparently self-contradicting subtleties of his moods'.

Two final extracts: The *Westminster Review* (July 1886) talked of the consummate art in describing places and persons, the aptness and pictur-esqueness of expression, all leading to an unmistakable Hardy tone. An American reviewer in 1892 tells of the serpent of pessimism constraining Hardy's wings and places Henchard as 'a remarkable character-study from the point of view of a psychologist or a sociologist but that does not make him a proper hero for a novel'. Is Henchard a case study or the victim of social forces only? What do you think the reviewer finds lacking in Henchard as a hero?

Subsequent criticism of the novel has tended to concentrate on the character of Henchard as an individual within the community or Henchard as a representative of the community. These views are much influenced by the theories of Freud and Marx. Henchard's character has been clinically analysed – is he a manic depressive, for example – and his portrayal seen as an example of Hardy's amazingly intuitive psychological understanding. 'A damned and self-destructive individualist', as one critic put it. Or is he more a symbol of the old order unable to adapt? With hindsight we see that Farfrae can represent economic progress looking to the development of the limited company and the rationalisation of an agricultural industry. Anthropological critics suggest parallels with the widespread myths asso-ciated with seasonal fluctuation, the sacrifice of the leader being necessary to ensure continuity and stability. Sociological criticism points to class distinction and rising and falling in the social system as major themes. Elizabeth-Jane succeeds admirably, Henchard rises but is too volatile to maintain a stable position. Each succeeding generation re-interprets the novel according to its own view of man in the community. What would you include in a review for tomorrow's readers?

REVISION QUESTIONS

The following questions are designed to direct your revision to significant aspects of the book. Answers should obviously contain as much quotation and direct reference to the text as possible. Do not be afraid to challenge or modify the inference contained in a question, provided that you support your disagreement with appropriate references.

1. Discuss the assertion that for all his faults Henchard deserved a better fate.

2. There is a great deal in his life to detest yet we are infinitely moved by his death. Illustrate how Hardy develops our sympathy for an apparently unpleasant character.

3. Hardy wrote that 'character is fate'. What do you think is meant by this and how far is Henchard's fate determined by his character?

4. Compare the characters of Elizabeth-Jane and Lucetta and discuss their importance in the novel.

5. How appropriate is it that the novel should end with the future life and thoughts of Elizabeth-Jane?

6. How far do you agree with the accusation that Farfrae is cold and mercenary?

7. How far is 'dramatic irony' important in the novel? Discuss one specific example of its use in detail.

8. Choose two dramatic incidents in the novel and show their importance to its development.

9. Discuss the use of letters and notes in the plotting of the novel.

10. Discuss the parts played in the novel by any two of the minor characters.

11. Of what significance are (a) High-Place Hall and (b) 'Peter's Finger' in the novel?

FURTHER READING

Whereas in the years immediately following his death there were comparatively few books published on Hardy, since the early post-war period there
has developed a veritable Hardy industry with a constant flow of books
and essays, some indispensable, some verging on the ridiculous. A personal
choice should include the following:

Biography

Hardy, Florence Emily, *The Life of Thomas Hardy*, Macmillan. Although
   published under his wife's name in two volumes, by far the greater part
   of the book was prepared by Hardy himself. We must remember that
   this is what Hardy wished us to know of his life and there are tantalising
   gaps. Nevertheless it remains an essential and fascinating source-book.
Millgate, Michael, *Thomas Hardy, A Biography*, Oxford. The most recent
   and most authoritative biography. Meticulously researched and presented.

General Works

Brown, Douglas, *Thomas Hardy: The Mayor of Casterbridge* (Studies in
   English Literature), Edward Arnold. An interesting and persuasively-
   argued study from one of the first sociological critics of Hardy. It has
   led to controversy.
Cecil, Lord David, *Hardy the Novelist*, Constable. A very readable general
   discussion of the novel.
Draper, R. P. (ed.), *Hardy, the Tragic Novels*, Macmillan. Casebook. This
   contains two good essays on our particular novel.
Howe, Irving, *Thomas Hardy*, Macmillan. A very sound general introduc-
   tion.
Millgate, Michael, *Thomas Hardy, his Career as a Novelist*, Bodley Head.
   This is among the very best of books on Hardy's fiction.
Pinion, Frank: *A Hardy Companion*, Macmillan. An invaluable reference
   work, covering all aspects of Hardy's work in meticulous detail.
Sumner, Rosemary, *Thomas Hardy, Psychological Novelist*, Macmillan.
   This contains a provocative essay on the character of Henchard in the
   light of recent research in the psychology of aggression.
Macmillan Casebook Series: *Hardy, The Tragic Novels*. This reprints two
   excellent essays, on character and on the sociological approach to the
   novel.